I'm In Love With An Entrepreneur!

HOW TO ENSURE YOUR RELATIONSHIP SURVIVES THE HIGHS AND LOWS OF ENTREPRENEURSHIP.

FREDERICK D. ACKLIN

ISBN: 978-1-965082-20-1

Publishing By:
DemiCo National, LLC
www.DemiCoNational.com

TABLE OF CONTENTS

FORWARD

Most books on new venture creation are relentlessly performative, giving guidance on how to complete a business plan. Dr. Frederick Acklin takes a different approach. Adopting the voice of an experienced and wise mentor, he guides the would-be entrepreneur/new venture creator through the wisdom process of identifying and selecting a partner, while also giving nuggets of wisdom and experience to those who will date an entrepreneur. He emphasizes what they need to know and why they need to know it by engaging and scholaring without being dry and demystifying the process.

This is a must-read for the Entrepreneur and Partner interested in dating an entrepreneur. Acklin presents an engaging and wide-range approach to dating an entrepreneur by managing expectations, and the precautionary methods before engaging in commitment as an entrepreneur or commitments unknown to those in pursuit of an entrepreneur.

It was exciting for me not because he is my best friend and brother, and I know his brilliant mind but also because he covers great content and context for those of us who are not novice to entrepreneurship, so this is amazing for those who are new to the game! Mindset, context, content, and the type of behaviors necessary for being an entrepreneur's partner is an untapped market, so this is definitely a "GAME CHANGER". The author also draws from a global selection of examples to show the universality of many entrepreneurial dating practices along with a set of recommended exercises to help the reader on their way."

Finally, a book of practical usage for the rest of us. A book not bound by the myths of the Silicon Valley, but rather a book that speaks to the entrepreneurial spirit in all of us. Acklin has put together a very practical book that is perfect for students, aspiring entrepreneurs, or any person with a desire to pursue an opportunity and to achieve a goal to have healthy relationships as we fight this battle and everyday chaos as an entrepreneur. This is a book for real people looking to create real successful relationships and real career partners that meet their goals, expectations, and dreams. It doesn't create mythical falsehoods. This book is going on the syllabus for sure."

Reading this book was a valuable refresher for me and a reminder of some of my many mistakes in the area of not just dating but relationships. If you are considering dating an entrepreneur, save yourself time, headache, heartache, stress, depression, anxiety and money by reading this first!"………… And if you are an entrepreneur, you already know!

—Brian Pleasant , CEO of Pleasant Global Enterprises and author of *" I F&$%ED Up on PURPOSE"*

INTRODUCTION

There are as many types of business families as there are colors in the sky. Business makes the world go round, but what happens on the other side of business? Everybody has a personal life outside of the office. Being a business owner, or the spouse of a business owner, can make for some less-than-traditional family issues. When I say business family, I mean families in which one or both of the heads of household own and/or run one or more businesses. The many different types of businesses create as many different lifestyles. What does that mean for those of us who are "married to the business"? We are the unsung heroes of this great economy.

Do you feel like you're married to the business? If you are the spouse of a business owner, then you most certainly are married to the business. The spouses of business owners are often those who stand at the ready, in the background, waiting for the other shoe to drop, or the ball to be thrown, whichever idiom you choose. We are all the "helpmates" of our partners. We are forever waiting, staring at the clock, for the phone call telling us our spouse made it safely to a business meeting across the country. We are regularly getting the kids through dinner, baths, and bedtime all on our own. We are consistently waiting up until all hours of the night for our spouse to get home after completing "one more thing" on their project.

To those of you out there who are entrepreneurs, you may know just how hard it is to find a partner who fits your goals and your perspective of life. As an entrepreneur, your entire life revolves around what you can do next to keep your business running or what other cool business ideas you could be involved in. Whatever is going on in your life, you always want more. You want to learn new skills, engage in all sorts of fun activities, and always look for something thrilling. And yet, that also means that finding someone who is willing to work with you in a partnership, someone who can "put up" with this extra excitement and will to always push yourself further, and someone who gets excited about it, is difficult. And so, this is why this book was created.

It is likely that many of you are not entrepreneurs. Perhaps you have started to date someone who works on their own business or who is always busy trying to leverage their social circle to try and come up with new business models and plans. Maybe you admire it, and maybe you love the person very much, but maybe you are also growing relatively tired of having to compromise all the time in a relationship. Of course, not all entrepreneurs are the same, but many have a few things in common: they are impulsive, ambitious, and oh so eternally busy.

Does going for a walk in the afternoon sound like a fun plan? Maybe for you, but your partner may be in her or his coworking space working on some cool new project. Want to go on vacation to a beautiful destination? Well, get ready to have them be on the phone or their laptop for a good amount of the time. Again, not all entrepreneurs are the same, and maybe your entrepreneur is the kindest, least impulsive person you know. However, there is a reason why you bought this book. This reason is probably because no matter what you do and how much you are trying to cope with certain small issues in your relationship, you have that icky feeling in your stomach that you need help to figure things out. There is nothing wrong with searching for help before something is completely broken.

Dating an entrepreneur is not impossible, nor is it something that will take the life out of you. Instead, it's an experience that can bring you to new levels of highs. Living with an entrepreneur means that you always get to hang out with someone who is positively minded and someone who sees opportunities in challenges. An entrepreneur always suggests cool new ideas and projects that you could be interested in, and they enjoy taking on new challenges. That means that when you come to them with a question or a worry, you can expect that they will put everything aside to help you find the best solution possible.

The reason I am writing this book is to reach out to those others who are married or dating the business owner. This book is meant to help frame conversations and family processes that will help strengthen and prepare the family unit for the best and worst that your business brings.

The major thing I have learned throughout these adventures is that the spouses of business owners and business starters must get on board with their significant other's need to build and grow businesses. Business owners/starters spend family money on ventures, assume the risk of failed ventures, work

80-hour weeks, spend weeks/months/years waiting on returns on investments, travel extensively, pay for their own health care etc. The spouses, meanwhile, must hold help everything else together. This is true from the biggest business family to the smallest family-owned restaurant. The whole family eats, sleeps, and breathes the business. It's a very stressful lifestyle that can be very hard to navigate.

The common causes of divorce include financial strain, neglect, lack of communication, and divergent goals. Other professions keep people away from home and preoccupy their thoughts, but they don't produce the toxic cocktail of resentment and anxiety created by putting the family's security constantly at risk. Then there's that green-eyed monster, Jealousy. Have you too suffered jealousy over the time, effort, focus that your spouse spends on his/her business? That's a marriage killer for sure."

Perspective is everything. For example, "if the entrepreneur insists he is acting in his family's interest, but the spouse believes he is acting in his own. One test of the entrepreneur's motivation is how much of the family's collective life he is willing to sacrifice with little payoff. The bottom line is that marriage takes work and building a business takes work. If you want the best of both worlds, it's important to respect each part of your life by giving it the focus and devotion it deserves. Give yourself the edge and clarity you need to stay on both tracks of having a fulfilling marriage and prosperous business."

Top reasons for divorce are money and sex. The stress of entrepreneurship is so great both money and sex are challenges. Let's learn from these mistakes. Let's decide not to be a statistic or a failure. Let's learn how to frame a conversation so that we can express our needs, fears, desires while also supporting our spouse in their dreams and aspirations. Are you ready to start the adventure of business-proofing your marriage?

In this book, we examine the protocols, policies, and procedures of the business centered family. I really want success for your family and your business! The whole point is that we learn to frame conversations and set up family processes that will strengthen your family unit so that it can weather the ups and downs of business. If you feel out of your depth in the business world, this book is meant to be a resource to help you navigate it. I make no guarantees, but I think it's a good place to start. Let's get to work!

Chapter One

Beauty & The Business

In 1991, Disney pictures released one of its most iconic animated films, *Beauty & The Beast*. Basically, the story followed a beautiful and naïve maiden named Belle as she went head-to-head with a scary beast who had imprisoned one of her family members. Through love, empathy, and compassion, Belle later realized that the one she thought was the beast was not the beast at all, and that very one became her greatest ally, protector, and lover. I am in no ways insinuating that your partner is a beast to be tamed. I am simply suggesting that entrepreneurship is the beast that left untamed will always be in opposition of your family goals. Just as Belle lost her father to the imprisonment of the beast, you don't want to lose your partner or spouse to the beast of entrepreneurship.

But is entrepreneurship really a beast? YES! That is one of the first things that you must understand. Entrepreneurship is a beast. Once you understand that entrepreneurship is a beast, you have to acknowledge that it takes a particular type of individual to enter the castle of the beast. You may have now found yourself in a relationship or marriage with one of those individuals battling or imprisoned by the beast. You may ask yourself. What is my role? Why do I feel overlooked? Am I being selfish? All of these may be questions that plague your thoughts daily. Don't fret. We're just getting warmed up. It is very possible for you and your loved one to create the skills and boundaries you need to no longer being in opposition of the beast but allowing the beast to serve your relationship and family as a protector.

Before we dive into what it's like to be in a relationship or marriage with an entrepreneur and the ways you can increase your chances of success, perhaps pointing out what entrepreneurs are, how their mindset works as well as their reasons why they aren't great at dating is important. This helps us figure out where we are starting from, and therefore, where we can be headed. Many people think entrepreneurship simply means owning their own business where the money just flows in effortlessly. Unfortunately, this is not the case. Even passive businesses still require a lot of time and attention from the founder to get the business up and running on its own. There is a lot of pre-planning and dedication for an entrepreneur. So, let's talk about entrepreneurship and all that it entails. It's not something everyone knows about, so let's expand on what that is first before diving into the rest of the book.

What is an entrepreneur?

Entrepreneurship pertains to the process of creating wealth by means of an invention or experiment. Usually, entrepreneurs experience the feeling that they have "created" something unique and have the foresight to see that it will have extraordinary value for many. For some, this is enough, although not always, they seek to expand their enterprise, and meet the needs of other customers by offering more and more products. Other than this requirement, there are basically no strict requirements for entrepreneurs, and even fewer criteria for what entrepreneurship is. It's simply a process of creating products or ideas that can solve problems. Entrepreneurs are usually self-employed individuals who generate their own income through some sort of business enterprise. They come up with new ideas or invest in something along with others, with the goal of making some profits. They do not necessarily control their businesses, but they can control the processes in certain ways. For some people, the thrill of the unknown inspires entrepreneurship.

And if entrepreneurship cannot fully be attributed to hard work and intelligence, one can also note that certain entrepreneurs possess skills that make them good business managers and able to apply their knowledge and skills to other ventures. Similarly, entrepreneurs will tend to struggle with personal relationships because of their way of making business out of everything-or seeing all interactions as 'deal making'.

The other defining characteristic of entrepreneurship is risk. In the world of venture capital, for example, and in the world of entrepreneurship in general, risks that lead to failure or mistakes can and do occur. Hoverer, because most of the risk occurs in the beginning stages of business operations, most entrepreneurs are used to taking these risks as they arise rather than waiting for them to occur. As a result, many new entrepreneurs are unprepared for major losses and financial catastrophes. In order to prepare for these things, many entrepreneurs have taken training courses to become more skilled in money management and in business development. By understanding and anticipating risks, entrepreneurs gain a higher degree of control over their ventures, which increases their chances for success.

Now, you may be wondering why I am explaining some financial stuff in a book about love, and understandably so. It's simple: entrepreneurs usually put their work at the center of everything. By understanding exactly what they do and therefore bow they work in business and finance, you can also understand why many times, they struggle with basic relationships. What may come naturally to you may not sound so 'normal' or 'obvious' to them. As they are used to taking a risk for a living, they may feel like their relationship is a series of risk-taking activities. To this end, you may end up feeling like your relationship is a rollercoaster. Entrepreneurship demands a specific type of mindset if one seeks to succeed, and while that mindset may be beneficial in business, it can be dangerous in relationships.

The traits of an entrepreneurial mindset are, in a nutshell, the absence of fear in taking risks and innovation, and the ability to accept failures gracefully. If your partner thinks of themselves as an entrepreneurial person, then it is imperative to understand just why entrepreneurial mindset is so critical for your loved one to thrive, and therefore why you may struggle with your relationship if you do not understand it. For those who embrace and promote entrepreneurialism, they will attest to its tremendous benefits, and its resultant happiness, both personally and professionally. For others, however, it isn't as successful because both parties have difficulty understanding the other sides viewpoints.

This mindset pertains to the entrepreneurial characteristics that successful entrepreneurs possess, including but not limited to the ability to work productively without much external interference, an uncanny ability to see visions and opportunities, an encyclopedic knowledge of and appreciation of the world around them, and a perspective of the world as something that can continuously be changed and made better. It is perhaps this mix of traits that makes the entrepreneurial spirit so attractive to so many people. And yet, for certain partne.rs, it may just feel overwhelming and may feel like the person they are with cannot stop and simply enjoy the present moment.

Being decisive is a definite characteristic of the entrepreneur.

Those who possess this trait are quick to make decisions, and take the steps needed to move their enterprises forward. Those who doubt their own abilities may be fearful of taking any risks, but those who see the opportunity and utilize the appropriate skills are much more successful. In short, those who possess the characteristics of being decisive will make the most of opportunities, taking risks, and being open to improvement. What this means for your relationship is that your entrepreneur partner may also be very open to doing anything possible to better your relationship. As such, although it may be annoying sometimes, it can also be the decisive factor in whether or not your relationship goes forward.

Those who truly embrace the entrepreneurial mindset also exhibit characteristics of resilience. Those with this mindset enjoy the work they do, recognize the hard work and dedication of others, and enjoy the recognition that comes with ongoing success. In short, entrepreneurs who value the strengths of their character and intelligence and cultivate a resilient mindset are resourceful and successful. Resilience is the ability to endure pain and the stress that inevitably comes with entrepreneurial challenges. Those with the resilience to change, learn, grow, and thrive are going to achieve exceptional results in their lives. Again, this means that although your relationship may be somewhat rocky and may have some fights, your partner is much more likely to be resilient and ready to do anything to keep the relationship going if he or she is dedicated to making your relationship work.

Finally, high-quality goals equate to success. Those who embrace entrepreneurial characteristics are driven by the need to be successful. To achieve high-quality goals means getting better and faster results, striving for the ultimate goal, and not settling. Therefore, you can feel good about being in this relationship- if they decide to be with you, it's because they really think it is worth putting time into it! They are dedicated to your relationship and that should feel amazing!

There are many reasons why a relationship with an entrepreneur may be difficult. As discussed above, they tend to have a very impulsive way of going about life for the simple reason that the edge of their seats, looking for ways to better every situation in their lives. Therefore, entrepreneurs are notorious for being questionable partners. They are also known for being devout leaders, and some of actually do well in business. However, when it comes to relationships, it's a different ball game! With a partner who always wants to lead, you may find yourself getting annoyed or frustrated because you may feel like you have a lack of control over the relationship. This is something that needs to be discussed by the two of you to make sure no one gets hurt in the process.

What does it mean to be dating or married to a business owner? Why is this a particularly challenging lifestyle? Every relationship has its challenges, and every family has its unique dynamics. I certainly do not want to be dismissive or minimize the issues related to main-stream lifestyles, but there is something about owning a business that ratchets up the strain on the family to another level. These issues are real, and they are documented. They do not discriminate, and they are not gender specific. Yet no one talks about it.

People often start companies to do their own things, while partnership is about doing things together. Particularly in already-strained relationships, there is no tension a business can't make worse. The core issue, it seems, is that being a business owner is a very lonely ambition and one that can cause the spouse to feel resentful, insecure, and terribly separate from their partner. If you don't feel connected to your spouse and don't share the ups and the downs of work, then you won't be sharing the load, both in the relationship and in the business. If the load is uneven for long, both the relationship and the business can fail.

Chapter Two

Proceed With Caution

While many of you reading this book are likely already in a relationship with an entrepreneur, I want to take a moment to speak to those who are still looking for that special someone. Let's be honest. Entrepreneurship is not only popular today, but also trendy. It seems that everywhere you look everyone is starting his or her own business, so if you're still looking for your soul mate, it's highly important that you consider the odds that he or she might just be an entrepreneur. Don't lose yourself in their charismatic smile, chiseled features, or the butterflies in your stomach. You need to know exactly what you're in for because signs of entrepreneurship may show up on the first date and if you're not prepared, you may mistake a text from a client as a text from another romantic partner.

Dating an entrepreneur is something that is likely to bring a lot of ups and downs in your relationship. Whatever happens, your partner is going to be going through moments of impulsivity when they feel they are on top of the world.

And then, the next day, they may receive a bad review on their business website, leaving them feeling low and as though they are moving towards nothing. This depends on the person's personality, of course, as some may be very growth-minded and see all mistakes or failures as opportunities to learn, while others may feel much more hurt by small mistakes. This is just one insight into your relationship but there are many more to learn. Here are a few expectancies you need to consider if you can handle.

Off the Clock? What's That?

As you may have gathered from the previous point, an entrepreneur's life is mostly ruled by a schedule. But even then, the schedule tends to be hectic and never truly ends. What this means is that your partner is very likely to stay at work most of the time. Now, that doesn't mean that you will need to go out on dates at the office and eat dinner there. Instead, what it does mean is that they rarely clock out. Your entrepreneur may have clients located all over the world. They may be working for Chinese clients, and in the morning, they have to be on the phone at 5AM to conduct a video conference with German stakeholders.

Therefore, they are likely to have a schedule that never ends. So, if you find your partner being on the phone all the time, or constantly speaking to people at all hours of the day, just keep in mind that this is only a part of who they are. They live for the thrill of never really stopping. If you feel like you are neglected in the relationship, point it out to them and try to find. a solution together that will work for the both of you. Of course, if this is just something that comes with the relationship, perhaps you need to reconsider your choice of dating this person. Or, better yet, become an entrepreneur too and share this passion!

Don't Make Me Choose!

Although you may be tempted to tell them that they need to choose between you and their entrepreneurial goals, the likelihood is that this will not work for them. The reason for this? Your partner's sole identity is led by the fact that he or she is an avid fan of pressure, adrenaline, and working nonstop. Being an entrepreneur is not a phase, it's a lifestyle, however cliche that may sound. If you expect them to change for you, and I am not talking about answering their messages to you faster or showering at a different time in the morning, your relationship is likely not to make it very far. Instead, try to compromise with one another. If you find that your partner is struggling with certain projects at work, try to offer help. If you see that they are getting a bit messy and are forgetting certain things, such as taking the trash out, doing their laundry, give them a helping hand.

Missing Important Events

Of course, you can't expect that your entrepreneur partner will miss out on your wedding or something very sentimental to you. If this is the case, either you choose together a time that works for both of you, and you are very well within your rights to choose to let go of the relationship. However, certain events like birthdays, big celebrations at work or your office's Christmas party may be missed because of the responsibilities that your significant other has. If this is something that truly bothers you, set up boundaries. Make it clear to your partner that you have certain expectations on social events. For example, choose together which celebrations cannot be missed, such as New Year's Eve or each other's birthdays. This will help you both avoid some heartache when the time comes to celebrations and your partner isn't able to show up. If they must cancel although you have both decided to spend a specific holiday together, do not feel guilty for voicing your disappointment. That's also a part of being an entrepreneur-living up to people's expectations!

All By Yourself

Alongside a very hectic schedule, your entrepreneur is also likely to have many trips to go through. Of course, during the Covid-19 pandemic, that wasn't exactly the case, and people may have thought that face-to-face travel

would be wiped off the map after a little while. Nonetheless, we are seeing a return to business travel. If your partner needs to travel often to meet clients, you can do two of the following: offer to come with them once in a while and make it a part-business part-vacation trip. Otherwise, you can also take the time to be with yourself and to enjoy your independence. This is likely to depend a lot on the frequency at which they travel and how comfortable you are being alone a lot of the time.

Of course, this also requires trust from both sides. You may be worried about your partner not being truthful, but a healthy relationship requires that the both of you trust one another to know that you love each other enough to be respectful of one another, even when you are apart.

High Highs and Low Lows

As mentioned above, entrepreneurs tend to change their minds and reactions rather often, sometimes making it difficult for the person they are dating to stay in the loop. If it's not related to the business, it may be related to your relationship. They tend to feel things very intensely and can change their mind or perspective of the relationship quickly, which can be overwhelming for some. For example, you may end up having a fantastic first date and feel like you really hit it off, but they may also realize during the date that they don't really have the time or energy to date at that specific moment. Therefore with entrepreneurs, it's important to be ready for more rock-and-roll than with other kinds of partners. This is also affected by age, however, so do not be surprised if your early twenties partner is even more all over the place.

The Struggle is Real

Entrepreneurs aren't all like Jeff Bezos or Mark Zuckerberg. Although an entrepreneur may be working 24/7, it does not necessarily mean that their business has already hit it off on the market. This means that you may be dating someone whose finances are also up and down, and therefore may need to settle for cheaper dates to accommodate them. This will naturally depend on the nature of their work and how advanced they are. But, in most cases, whenever entrepreneurs are at the starting point of their career, they are juggling all kinds of investments while also working on creating new businesses, all while still having bills to pay. It can take years before a business 'makes it'. If you're happy with that and want to provide a supporting hand, or the mental support they will need through rough times, go for it! You're in for a great experience. The loyalty that emerges in your relationship from having been there throughout the entire process is unlike anything else.

Quiet Time

When you think of an entrepreneur, what do you think of? Perhaps you imagine someone jumping around from one conference to the next trying to secure funding. Maybe you think of the person who always talks to others to pitch their idea, while welcoming positive (and sometimes negative) feedback. Both are very true. In most cases, entrepreneurs are very extroverted people who like sharing their ideas as often as possible. However, that also means that once they come home, they are tired and just need to be on their own. They need solitude sometimes, and it's not because they're cheating. They just want to be alone-and that includes without you, even if it hurts. They might use their gym time as their alone time, which is why they'll shrug if you ask to go together. Again, we're back to the concept of boundaries. You need to put them up to make sure they know when their alone time becomes too much for you; for example, if you end up not spending any time together. If that's the case, they may rethink whether a relationship is the right thing for them at that specific time.

Crazy Schedule

If you have ever dated an entrepreneur, you'll know exactly what a hectic schedule looks like. Sometimes, especially at the beginning of the business or project the entrepreneur is working on, time spent at work may exceed twelve, fourteen, or sometimes even sixteen hours a day! In order to really make a profit or to really advance in their business, they may end up having to spend extra hours, nonstop, to see progress. A nine-to-five schedule therefore really fits what they need to do to see progress. When dating someone who works like this, it can end up feeling lonely. Meeting your friends in the evening with your partner may not be possible because they need to be up the next day early for client calls. Or, going out of town for a weekend might not be possible because there is no internet.

They will also often work on weekends to make sure they don't miss out on opportunities. But don't get this wrong, they love doing it! So, this passion is something you can share with them. Similarly, as they have a hectic schedule, you just need to fit into it. By planning in advance, you can enjoy quality time together. So, spontaneous lovers out there, dating an entrepreneur may feel like you are imprisoned unless you figure out how to fit your schedule around this. You may also feel like they are 'scheduling you in' like they would a client, but it is not because this is how they see you. Instead, it's just how it works out for them, and it's their way of showing the care and love they have, and they want to fit someone important to them in their busy schedule because they know that if they don't, they will only see one thing: you, walking away.

Talking Too Much?

On the same line of ideas, entrepreneurs like to talk to people. A lot. They are very curious and see an opportunity whenever they think there may be one. They take chances and they know that networking is everything. Because of this, it isn't unlikely that they start up conversations with just about anyone and everyone in all kinds of settings. This may be making you uncomfortable at times, especially if you struggle to spend time alone with one another without distractions. More so, you may feel like your partner is flirting with everyone he or she meets, but this is rarely the case -especially in front of you! And even so, sometimes, in order to strike a deal, one has to bat one's eyes a little bit more. It doesn't mean anything, really. It's just business. Similarly, they may want to learn from people and experience a lot of different people and their past, so if they strike up a conversation with someone when the two of you are at a bar, don't think too much of it. Join in on the conversation instead of staying in your corner, and your entrepreneur will feel like the luckiest person in the world to have someone like you on their side ready to share their passion!

Feeling Unseen

An entrepreneur has made it this far because they are able to turn an entire room around them and can bring themselves to the biggest table simply by striking up a conversation with the right people. Similarly, as part of their job (and personality, let's be honest!), they get in on the conversation by also bringing a lot of attention to themselves. They get in the spotlight a lot of the time because their brain is wired to be ready to pitch their idea to the next person that comes, especially because they are used to taking up any opportunity that comes to them. As such, it may happen that you are with a partner who ends up taking all the space in a restaurant or at a convention. You need to make sure that your partner is aware of this trait if it makes you feel uncomfortable whenever you are surrounded by people and you feel like you can' t place a word in. Your partner may have to go the extra mile to make sure you are included in the conversation, but you can also play your part by sharing your stories and perspectives.

Likable... and dislikable.

Whenever you meet someone who is very loud and who takes up a lot of space in a conversation, usually, the reaction is one of the following two: you are either very impressed with this person and how they manage to have all this confidence, or you are turned off by what seems to be an unhealthy amount of arrogance. The same is true for most people, including your friends and family who may feel like your partner is not the right one for you. Usually, the response you get in regards to your relationship is based on how your partnership is. For example, your partner may be loved by your family because they have inspired you to create your own business and you are now both at the best place you could be in your life. Otherwise, your friends and family may hate your partner because they are taking up all the space and attention in your relationship, leaving you with very little attention or care. Your family and friends, however, may not understand your relationship. Perhaps they are only used to knowing what it is like to date someone who works a 9-to-5, or maybe they do not know exactly how to feel about the fact that most of your interactions take place either during work or in between two gigs, meetings, or calls. If this is something you are comfortable with, then make sure to make it clear with your friends and family. They will appreciate hearing your side of the story and making sure that you are happy in this situation!

Arguments

In order to make it as an entrepreneur, you often have to be very clear on your opinions, what you think works for a business, and what you think needs to be changed. You need to be a gamechanger, and oftentimes, you have to go against the status quo. Not only this, but entrepreneurs must be able to support and defend their points at all times, the same way they need to know how to convince other people (for example investors) that the project or product they are working on has the potential to become profitable. As such, it isn't rare that an entrepreneur will have to work through their ways of going about conflict They are passionate people, and they love what they do. It can, however, become problematic if you feel like you cannot go against what they say is right or wrong. Be sure to know the difference between productive and toxic conflict (the latter being where your opinions and perspectives are being ridiculed or set aside). You can also mention this to them, explaining that you understand why they may need to stand by their convictions, but that a conflict with their partner can be a different story.

Attracted to Energetic People

Because they themselves are very energetic and driven people, they also like being surrounded by people who have the same energy and vibe as they do. Because of this, you will often find that with individuals who aren't very certain about what they do -or who have absolutely no drive or ambition to do anything specific -do not end up in very successful relationships. Laziness is potentially one of the worst traits in people, according to entrepreneurs. The latter see their life as being something you only get to live once, and therefore something that you should try and do the most possible.

Hence, being lazy is something that usually brings the relationship to an end rather quickly. Being lazy does not mean watching Netflix once in a while or needing time off. What it means is choosing not to work because you don't feel like it or limiting your own potential for no reason. The relationship may end up being very one-sided and if the non-entrepreneurial partner is indeed somewhat lazy, they may feel as though every conversation turns into the entrepreneur trying to teach them how to live their life. Of course, this makes for a very short-lived relationship as no one likes to feel like they are always being told to change, which is why they are usually not a great match for any entrepreneur.

No Drama.

This is not to say that your entire relationship should revolve around your capacity to keep the partnership interesting. Instead, it is more about understanding how entrepreneurs' function. Entrepreneurs will often have fifteen projects going on at the same time. No matter what they are doing, they want to be learning, growing, and bettering themselves. Stagnation and 'normalcy' sound like the worst possible outcome to them. In other words, your relationship should be one where you both grow and become better people together. An entrepreneur wants a relationship that will compliment his or her life, something that he or she can enjoy while growing more and more successful. As such, if you are looking for a relationship that is calmer, more stable, and that offers a solid plan for the future, or if you want a relationship where you always know what is coming up next, dating an entrepreneur is most likely not your best option.

Ultimately, these are the fifteen main things to understand whenever you are dating an entrepreneur. It is a very exciting journey, and especially one that will either end up being fantastic and wonderful to live through, or one that will leave you rather brokenhearted. If it doesn't work out with the entrepreneur, do not feel like it is your fault. We each have our own ways of living our life, and perhaps you want more stability or calmness. But since you are here reading this book, I suspect that this isn't the case! As such, let's discuss a way that you can keep your relationship going, especially when things get hard.

Chapter Three

The 5 Love Languages

Before we go further into the world of entrepreneurship and romantic relationships, it is first needed for you to understand how to function just in a romantic relationship. If your skills as a romantic partner are lacking, then the likelihood that you'll survive in a relationship with an entrepreneur is slim to none. Yes, your partner may be a business minded guru, but he or she is still a human with precise methods in which they process and receive love.

Falling in love is magical and can be described as euphoric and exciting, but how do you keep love alive? This is the tricky part. As your relationship advances, you and your partner will go through different seasons of life. The task is to find ways to stay in love despite the changes you will inevitably experience. I believe it is essential to determine your love language in all relationships.

Whether your relationship is flourishing or failing, it's important to communicate how you would like to receive love and ho\v your partner wants you to show love. Speaking different languages makes it harder to fall in love and meet each other's emotional needs. Decide if your love language will be affirmative words, quality time, gifts, actions, or physical contact, and start by keeping your partner's love alive and making sure it will last a lifetime.

So, what is the right formula to a lasting marriage? Even with many experts, books, and studies on marriage, couples continue to struggle to make their Jove last. Maybe couples don't work out because they don't understand how relationships go through different stages. For example, the first phase that a new couple goes through is the attraction phase and is classified by a feeling of euphoria.

During this stage, we feel so in love and believe it will be forever. We want to be together day and night, and we can't imagine that anything could ever come between us. This step allows us to see our world through rose-colored glasses and hides our judgment. But how long does this phase last? I believe that this romantic obsession can't be a long-lasting feeling and only lasts for around two years. It may take more than two years if the relationship is secret; But when this stage is over, we often return to earth and begin to see the opposing sides of our partner that we formerly ignored.

Well, how do you make love work after this phase? The truth is, you have to stop obsessing over the idea of being "in love." Instead, true love disappears, and we have to work hard to keep our relationships afloat. The goal is not to feel "in love" but to feel truly loved by another person. That is to say; we need to feel worthy of love and work with emotional communication that can support the relationship. It's time to embrace a new mindset, set your expectations from your partner, and lay the foundation for a successful relationship.

Have you ever wondered what happens to love after marriage? It's a common question people ask. However, the answer is far from easy. Just as people speak different languages such as English or Mandarin, they also speak different languages of love. Think of the language of love as the language you speak. For example, suppose you speak English, and your partner speaks Mandarin. How will you communicate? In order to be able to speak deeply with each other, one must also learn the other language. This also applies to the language of love, but unlike learning another language, learning your language of love is a bit ambiguous and takes a bit more effort. The word "love" is a confusing term. We use it all the time to describe the foods we love, like tacos and ice cream, as well as the activities we participate in, like jogging or dancing. But what does love mean to you' To answer this question, I want to suggest looking back at your childhood. Child psychologists have shown that children have an emotional need to be loved and valued, and the consequences of not meeting those needs can lead to emotional instability. Moreover, this emotional instability can lead to actions against their parents and even their partner later in life.

Think of your emotional needs as a tank of love, similar to your car's fuel tank. Just like your car can't run without fuel, you can't run without love. If you keep the love tank full, your "car will run smoothly, but you can start to be self-destructive if you let love go away. Keeping the tank full is essential in any marriage and learning the language of love from your partner has the power to change their behavior and your relationship dramatically.

Words Of Affirmation

How do you always feel when you get an accolade or a compliment? You are probably feeling good, and that makes your day a little better, doesn't it? Well, some people need to hear these compliments from their partners. Their love language is affirmation words, and they only want to hear positive, empowering words from their partner. It can be a little compliment or even a simple thank you for something you have done. Start with words of encouragement. By encouraging your partner, you start to be motivated. So, if you notice that your partner wants to try something new, you can back them up with words of encouragement and push them in the direction they want. It's essential to keep your partner's best interests first when encouraging them to do what they want to do. Read my book, *I Always Put My Mouth On Her.*

Take for example, if you want your partner to get a better-paying job, your pep talk can have the opposite effect. Of course, your words can be disappointing if they don't want to change either. But if you are encouraging them to develop a new skill or talent, now is an excellent time to use affirmative words to show your support for your partner.

Then use kind words even when you're feeling angry and living in the past. There's no point blaming your partner for things that have happened before; instead, I suggest that you leave the mistakes behind and live in the present. Forgive your partner and build a positive environment in which to exchange nice words, even when dealing with small tasks like doing the dishes and laundry.

Using humble words is also crucial in a relationship. You need to avoid asking your spouse for things, or your relationship can become a parent-child dynamic instead of a partnership. Instead, ask your partner for something that will make them feel affirmed and generous. For example, imagine someone complained that her husband still hadn't painted his room after nine months of asking him to! I think that she compliments him every time he did something she liked instead of asking him to paint the room. Although he was skeptical at first, his client tried this technique. What happened? Just three weeks later, her husband was painting the room. The trick is to focus on compliments from your partner rather than criticizing them.

Quality Time

In our today's world, we are busier than ever. We split our time between work, family, friends, and personal care. We live busy lives, and quality time has become a precious commodity. When we return home from a long day at work, we can spend the evening eating, putting the kids to bed, and watching shows or news on Television. But I want to point out that sitting on the couch and watching TV is not a good time. So, what's the key to spending time together? Unrivaled attention.

With innumerable distractions from our smart devices, it can be challenging to pass the time without interruption, Quality time is about spending ti.me with each other and focusing on your partner, not just being in the same room. Instead, the secret behind quality time is focused attention. Instead of looking into the other person's eyes all the ti.me, you need to give your partner your full attention. For example, you can go on a date, take a walk, or even cook a meal together. This kind of quality time enables you to share love, respect, and appreciation for each other.

Take Rita and Jason, for example, who spend quality time in the bookstore. While Rita loves to flip the shelves for her next book, Jason helps her out, although he does not share the same appreciation for literature. Plus, the two created a compromise that works. Rita has learned to minimize her time looking for books when she sees Jason's anger building up. Jason thanks Rita for not taking long to pay for her books.

Quality time can likewise be a simple conversation together. It is not enough to exchange words; instead, couples who are having a good time maintain eye contact while their partner talks, actively listen, pay attention to their partner's feelings, and make sure they don't interrupt. You also need to identify your partner's personality type. Maybe you fall into the Dead Sea category, where you listen intently but don't join the conversation. Or perhaps you are the "babbling brook" that has to pour its thoughts into a constant stream of words. Often these extreme personalities get married; However, these types of people become irritated and exhausted when the euphoria of the relationship dwindles. If your relationship follows this pattern, I believe that you have a "minimal daily need" to share three things a day with your partner in order to keep both parties happy.

Receiving Gifts

People who love gifts may seem materialistic, but that isn't necessarily true. Receiving gifts has long been a part of Mayan culture and is simply a way to deposit your love into something you can see. Gifts can take many forms, whether expensive, free, bought in stores, or even handcrafted. In fact, the gift itself isn't that important; the act of giving is what matters most.

For instance, if your partner speaks the language of gifts, any gifts you give them will be understood as physical representations of your love. The monetary value isn't as important as planning a gift, buying, or making, and finally presenting the gift makes the person feel so special and loved. Let us take a look at Bruce and Grace. You know, Bruce was buying gifts for Grace until they got married, and he quit. Grace's love language was receiving gifts, and by the time the gifts ran out, Grace felt emotionally abandoned. When asked why he stopped giving Grace gifts, Bruce simply explained that it was too much money. Since the value of money isn't important, Bruce began showering Grace with gifts of love and mending the relationship. Bruce learned the love language of Grace, and she felt valued and loved again.

Finally, if your partner's love language is receiving gifts, think of those gifts as small investments in your relationship. It will change the way you regard the cost of gifts. Remember, a gift can be as small as picking up your spouse's favorite candy from the grocery store on the way home. I suggest giving gifts regularly. Whether every day or weekly, your relationship needs to be consistent to benefit from the gifts.

Acts Of Service

Your partner may constantly ask you to do the dishes, fold the clothes, or fill up the car with fuel. In this case, your partner's love language is likely to be an act of service. To complete the acts of service, you need to do things for your partner that don't take a lot of time but have the power to have a considerable positive impact on your marriage.

We can take a closer look at a couple who both spoke the language of acts of service but couldn't be happy with each other. The problem was not that they didn't speak different languages, but that they spoke different dialects. In other words, the couple did many things for each other, but not the things the other thought was the most important. To resolve the problem, the couple wrote down the most important things to them so that they could speak the same language again.

When couples start to challenge each other, they begin their path to failure. Additionally, when deciding acts of service, you may need to adjust your perspective on traditional gender roles. For example, doing housework and raising children isn't just for women. Instead, regardless of stereotypical gender roles, you need to define each other's responsibilities and decide what makes you happy.

Take the example of Tim, who grew up in a family where his father believed that housework and chores like changing diapers were just for women. Yet, despite Tim's education, Tim knew that housework was essential to keeping his wife, Amanda, happy. Therefore, he let go of gender stereotypes of his childhood in other to make Amanda feel loved and respected in return.

Physical Touch

Research proves the importance of physical touch in examining infants who were held and kissed often versus those who were not. Those who have experienced more physical touch led healthier emotional lives, and many crave the same physical touch later in their partner's life. Suppose your partner's love language is physical touch. In that case, it can be easy to communicate through simple acts like kissing and holding hands or even acts like sex. It can be conveyed by more complex actions, such as a massage, which requires time.

Ultimately, it's essential to learn how your partner would like to be physically touched in order to speak their language. Take, for example, Naomi, who married a soldier who spent time overseas. With the departure of her partner to the army base, Naomi was unable to receive any physical touch that made her feel loved and valued. Yet, despite his absence, Naomi found a way to feel close to her husband by wearing his clothes or sending him pictures. So even in the absence of the other, it's essential to find ways to connect and speak each other's love languages.

Many couples find it important to explore and communicate with each other in a way that they enjoy speaking the language with physical touch. In fact, both parties need to express how they want to be touched and take the time to meet the needs of the other. It is also important to ask for feedback. Remember, you are just learning to speak their language. So, whether you're just keeping your hands on the couch or kissing your partner goodbye or hello, showing your love every day doesn't take a lot of effort.

Determining Your Love Language

Now that you've discovered the top five love languages, how do you know which one is right for you? Ask yourself, "What do you want the most? The solution to this question might not be easy; luckily, there are other ways to determine which language of love matters to you the most.

First of all, ask yourself what you ask the most from your spouse. The things you desire from her the most are probably the ones that fulfill you emotionally. What makes you feel good It might be when your partner cooks a meal, does the dishes, or even buys a gift. Once you've decided what's right for you, you can start figuring out your love language. Then you have to ask yourself what your partner is doing that is hurting you the most.

If you find out how much your partner causes you pain, knowing how your spouse causes you pain can guide you in finding out your love language. After answering these questions, you will discover that you respond to one or more of these languages. A lot of people will have more than one love language; just as many people are bilingual, one can undoubtedly be bilingual in love too. It just means that your partner will have more opportunities to communicate love with you.

Not only do you have to think about the fact that your previous romantic relationships didn't love you, but you also have to think back to your childhood to find out why you feel love the way you do. For example, Erica's love language is receiving gifts. She remembers spending Christmas morning opening gifts from her brother, who found random items in the house to give to her. Unfortunately, he didn't take the time to find gifts for the people he loved, and Erica remembered how that made her feel unloved and unappreciated. This experience made Erica realize how important it is for her to receive gifts.

Once you've determined your main love language, rank the other four based on their weight. Then, ask your spouse to do the same and compare your answers. By discoursing your love languages, you and your partner can work to fill each other's tanks of love. I suggest that you and your partner sit down three times a week for three weeks and examine how full your love tank is and what you can do to fill it. After all, communication is the key and the cutting edge of a successful marriage.

When two people get together and married, their love changes. They no longer feel the passion and euphoria they once had, but that doesn't mean a relationship has to end. Every relationship goes through the phase where reality strikes, and each partner must decide if they are ready to go the distance. Everyone should also realize that going the distance takes time, effort, and a lot of communication.

Marriage is hard work but learning each other's love language can make things easier and help you show love to your partner. Whether it's speaking affirmation words, spending time together, receiving gifts, having physical touch, or completing acts of service, you can better understand how to communicate with your partner and speak each other's loving language. The point is to keep your love tank filled and to communicate with each other when the tank seems empty. By learning your love languages, you can work to fill your love tanks and have an emotionally fulfilling relationship that will run smoothly forever. No amount of support that you offer to your partner's vision or business dreams will make a difference if you are offering such in a way that is not their love language.

Chapter Four

I'm All In

Once you've tallied up the cost of being in the relationship with an entrepreneur and you decide to proceed, then it is time to start building the framework of a healthy relationship. "Love" has various different connotations. On the one hand, it is a pure, abstract attraction which exists almost as a vacuum without any involvement of other people. Then again, love is described as a burning flame that consumes everything in its path and demands complete commitment. In between these two lies a middle area, which is where dating takes place.

The most common form of love is passionate love, which occurs when couples are just starting to feel emotionally connected and are experiencing a heightened sense of attraction and closeness between the two of them. The more attached a couple becomes to their partner the greater the emotional support they feel. Couples who love deeply and know how to show it are likely to have deeper connections to their partners than others. This type of love is also the most difficult to sustain and, if the couple loses this emotional support, it is likely that they will part ways. The level of commitment required to maintain a passionate love relationship is also the hardest for couples to maintain. This is often where relationships with entrepreneurs go wrong-the entrepreneur becomes too busy or not dedicated enough to a relationship and therefore lets the flame go out.

The second, and less common form of love, is compassionate love. Compassionate love occurs when a person loves someone not just because they are nice to them, but because that person is a good person and the love, they feel is due in large part to the person's kindness. A caring person can have the same effect on another person, as does a person who is purely in love with themselves (when a partner feels like they need someone to be happy). While this form of loving someone is rarely found in conventional relationships, it can arise and be sustained in many relationships. These tend to create uneven relationships where one person is more admiring and caring for the other, leaving this person feeling like they aren't being supported enough.

The last, and least understood form of love is unconditional love. Unconditional love means that you love your partner without condition, expectations, desires, etc. When you truly love someone in this manner, you are giving them all of your time, energy, emotional support, etc without expecting anything in return. People often think of unconditional love in terms of one-time gestures when they really mean long-lasting, nurturing relationships. While giving someone this kind of attention can often mean more in the beginning, in the long term, it can also become toxic if the receiving partner is not reciprocating the feelings. This is also why unconditional love tends to take place more in families.

When it comes to entrepreneurs, it can be easy to fall in love with someone for the image they show and the great things they accomplish. However, falling into these kinds of love patterns can also turn out to be more toxic than anything else. This is also why the partner's commitment to a relationship is a key indicator of how the relationship is going altogether. If your partner seems to be giving very little into the relationship, this may be a sign that both partners need to discuss boundaries and expectations. Similarly, a key point to make here is that the amount of time and attention being given to the relationship is also a tell-tale sign of how the relationship is really doing. So, how can you date someone who's busy? In the next section we will dive deeper into answering that question.

Setting Boundaries

Often, we think of boundaries as something that pushes us back or drives us away from people. But, healthy boundaries within relationships are often a prerequisite to happiness. They clearly define what's necessary and desirable in relationships and what isn' t.

Boundaries can help establish harmony within relationships. As a rule, it's important that each partner knows his or her own personal boundaries before establishing any with another. This way, once set, they can be looked at from a logical point of view and will make it easier to communicate about what needs to happen within the relationship. This is key when it comes to dating someone who is busy knowing what your boundaries and making these clear will also help your partner know when they need to act a certain way and whether they are crossing the line. For example, if spending less than three evenings together a week is a limit you do not want to cross, make it clear.

Boundaries are an important part of physical, mental health, and emotional well-being. They also keep people in their comfort zone which is something that is difficult for entrepreneurs. Therefore, they may struggle to conform within a set line of boundaries where you say "this is okay, and this isn't", but you also should make sure to make it clear that there are certain expectations. These will help your entrepreneur partner figure out what's acceptable in business, and what isn't in your relationship. When boundaries are not clearly set, people may feel freewill to do things they would not do if there were clear rules.

Setting Expectations

Arguably one of the most important things to do as a couple is to establish boundaries, as mentioned above, but also expectations for one another. If you are both entrepreneurs, the likelihood is that you'll both have to work on making time for each other. This can also mean spending time working on your business together and calling this quality time.

As long as you both work on making things fit your own schedules and on having time for each other in a way that works for both of you, you're good to go! As such, setting your expectations clearly also means that your partner needs to know what you want and how you want it. For example, you may want to start by being more casual about the whole relationship. If that means going on many lunch and coffee dates in between meetings, then so be it. For this, you need to be ready to accept that this is how the relationship will work in order to start. Therefore, that means knowing that you will be with someone busy and that you may want to keep yourself busy too. There is no point in being with someone if you feel like you are constantly waiting for them to be ready for you. It will make you feel bad about yourself and your accomplishments! Being casual will help you gauge whether this is something that you see yourself doing for the next few months or even years. You will also be able to get to know the person a lot more which can help you uncover baggage, potential red flags and to figure out whether this person really is someone you can imagine yourself with for the following years.

Next up, be realistic about your expectations. If you are already in a relationship with an entrepreneur, perhaps this applies less to you. But if you are dating, be realistic and remember that you may be leading two completely different lives with different priorities and ways of living. Concretely, this means that the person you are getting into a relationship with may not be available all the time and that you must be okay with this. A good way of dealing with it is simply to make yourself unavailable too! It makes coping with a busy person much better-you can both focus on your own things, but together. Communication is key to avoid disappointment.

Communication

Communication is important in any relationship, but when put under pressure the tendency is to either blow up or clam up. You may be surprised to find that you are not the only one struggling. Be patient with yourself and with your spouse. Like anything worth doing, this will take time and a lot of elbow grease. Communication is the key to a happy and successful relationship. But sometimes communication can be difficult, and it takes both parties to effectively share their thoughts and perspectives on a certain topic. Oftentimes, we hear how important communication really is, but we never really understand what communication means and how to use it in relationships. We learn communication through our social interactions with friends and families that we trust and depend upon. Relationships are built on communication in this same way, but unlike family, unconditional love is rarely present. Therefore, we must be able to know when we need to share our point of view and our feelings, even if it means that the other person may feel slightly hurt.

At the very root of it, communication is nothing more than the exchange of information through the means of voice (speaking), sight (body language), or feelings {emotions displayed, such as crying). Communication is therefore the combination of verbal and non-verbal cues and other ways of conveying a message to one another. The ability to communicate plays an integral part in the success of the relationship because it is truly the only way you have of making yourself heard. Your partner cannot know that something isn't working out or that their busy schedule makes you feel unloved and unwanted unless you tell them! A couple that does not communicate regularly will eventually drift apart and will have less chance of growing closer over the years.

Relationship communication is as much a part of building a relationship as it is a part of maintaining that relationship. Most of us do not like to talk about ourselves, particularly in front of other people. You do not always have to use words to communicate with each other. In some cases, you can convey your feelings through non-verbal communication and this makes all the difference in how effective communication is in a relationship. As long as your partner can get your point, you have achieved your goal. Communication does not only mean speaking your thoughts to each other but also listening to each other. Therefore, when you date someone busy, you have no choice but to make sure you communicate how you feel about this. Make time for the person, but only do so if they also make time for you.

You should not be feeling like a burden or as though you are only providing them with what they need when they need it, without anything in return. To recap, dating someone busy can be alleviated if you communicate properly, set up boundaries and expectations, and make the most out of the small meetings and time in general that you spend with this person. There are many more tips like these to know and prepare for before you date an entrepreneur, so let's discuss them in more detail. We will dive further into communication and tools that you may find useful later.

Business Proofing Your Relationship

This is a tricky chapter. Because we are all different, our relationships are different, our challenges are different, and our relationships are different. What works in other relationships might not work for you. However, three things remain the same:

1. We are all in a relationship with a business owner
2. The winding, tricky path to relationship happiness is fraught with peril

3. Divorces happen everyday

It goes without saying that neither building a business nor sustaining a happy marriage is easy--and trying to do both at once can seem an impossible dream. In fact, to hear some experts tell it, entrepreneurial couples need coping skills that regular people can hardly imagine. It seems that despite the pitfalls, plenty of entrepreneurial couples are meeting that challenge, and that, ironically, the shared struggle of creating a company can make a good established marriage even better.

For one thing, there's no evidence that the divorce rate among business owners is any higher than average (although when entrepreneurs do call it quits, the results can be a bit messier). Moreover, according to a recent survey by the investment advisory firm Neuberger Berman, 42°/o of CEOs of fast-growing startups say that running their own companies has had a positive effect on their relationships with spouses or domestic partners. That is significantly higher than the 32°/o who said business ownership had caused trouble on the homefront."

That all sounds pretty optimistic, doesn't it? We CAN do this and be successful in both our businesses and our marriages, but we have to be deliberate! Because, on the other side of these happy marriages and thriving businesses are the ones who fail. In fact, entrepreneurs are like everyone else who divorces.

They vow to do things differently next time. Many accept blame for having skewed priorities and promise their future spouses undivided attention. They talk about date nights and shared hobbies. The next marriage -- like the next company -- will benefit from lessons learned in the failure of the first. Remember, this is a PARTNERSHIP! You must make time for one another and remind each other that you are there for support as well as success.

At the beginning of every year sit down and decide what our goals are for that year. List personal, business, family, spiritual, health, and financial goals. Then break the year up into quarters and hold each other accountable. Sit down with your businessperson! Have a family business meeting and discuss the regrets of the past, the now, the future, and the road to get there. Ask questions and make him/her give you those answers. LEARN about your business and you will also be learning about your business owner. I PROMISE it will get easier with time and practice.

So, who drives your bus? Are you both fighting over who gets to hold the map, while your bus heads off a cliff? If so, put the brakes on now! Yes, it's hard to give up making all the decisions when you're the one who's used to it. Yes, it's hard to step out in faith about a financial question when you have no idea where the money will come from to pay for these dreams. Part of the goal setting process is establishing roles. That doesn't mean there's never any overlap. No one chairman makes the decisions in a business setting. There's a board of chairpersons in place to weigh the options and set the course. The same principles apply here.

Business Proofing Your Time Off

You have to help your partner with this process. One of the last things that any business owner wants to hear is that it's time to turn off that brain and focus on other parts of their lives. That's hard, right? You have put all your focus and time and effort into growing this wonderful business, and now you want me to think about something else? In short, YES!

There is life outside of the business. You have friends, family, children, animals, etc. that all need and deserve your attention. Even Bill Gates takes a vacation sometime. Richard Branson has a story in "Business Stripped Bare" where he is on safari in Africa with his family. Everyone is around a fire hanging out near a pride of lions. He was sitting in the truck on a satellite phone missing everything. Whether it's for an hour or a week, every business owner needs to be able to step back and focus on the things that aren't business related. Remind your business owner that he/she has other things that matter to them too. They should call their mom or play golf with their brother. They should take a nap on a lazy Sunday. They should be able to come up with conversations that don't always revolve around the business. It's important to long-term success as a person, not just a business owner, to be well-rounded. Play time (otherwise known as relaxation) is critical to creative thinking, problem solving, and a general sense of well-being. Choose a day or an hour a week. Schedule it and keep that appointment to yourself. The business, and the relationship, will benefit from it.

Chapter Five

Calming The Chaos

Entrepreneurs, although their lives tend to revolve around following a specific set of guidelines, deadlines and meeting schedules, are very (VERY) scattered. For the mental health of you and your [partner it will be of great benefit to help them organize and calm the chaos in their professional life. They want to do everything all at once because everything is exciting to them. That new project taking off, however, might take their attention away from something else which is very important, just like they may get lost in the number of tasks that they need to complete. However, as a partner, you can also help them find their priorities, drea.ms, and get more stability in their lives. Although it is true that they are most comfortable when things are hectic and all over the place, any human being needs to have some kind of stability in their lives. This is something you can help with! And, interestingly enough, it is also something that can help the both of you get closer to one another.

Establishing priorities might be a very difficult task to do with your entrepreneur. Why? Because to them, everything is a priority. Everything needs to get done in a timely manner, no matter what the task is. As such, and this is especially true when they are involved in numerous ventures all at the same time, an entrepreneur may struggle to find out what exactly they should be focusing on first before they start jumping onto the next project. Similarly, they will need your help to list out every single thing that they have going on and figure out exactly how they should be focusing their efforts and where they should be taking a few steps back. There are certain tools that they can use in order to get themselves organized, but one of the first tasks you may have on your list is to humble them a little bit.

Now, I know how this sounds: condescending. But it's true! Often, entrepreneurs will feel like they are the best to figure out their time and their commitments. And yet, they also often end up being the ones who are behind on their work, or they get lost in the sea of commitments that they have signed up for. Therefore, before you do anything to help, make sure that they want the help. If you already feel like they are going to be arguing with you the entire time, remind them that this is something you are doing to help them out, and nothing else! Once that's done, you can get started with the following steps:

Consolidate the tasks. How long is that going to take? Most entrepreneurs are very scattered because whenever an opportunity presents itself, they feel like they have no option other than to say yes and go ahead with it. What this means is that they probably have around fifteen different folders, time management apps, as well as project management apps that each have projects and ideas listed in no particular order. Therefore, the first step in setting priorities is making sure that everything is under the same exact folder. Get them to first list exactly what it is they need to be getting done. If that means using automation so every single message they receive ends up in the same in box, then so be it. Whatever works best for them to receive all messages into one place is going to be the best option. Some people work best with a pen and paper, while others may work much better with a digital version.

Now, you should guide your partner through the following four categories: what needs to be done now, what can be deferred to later, what can be delegated, and what can be deleted. This is prioritizing, and fine tuning can be done later. So, don't let your partner try and discuss each task, try to get him or her to just choose a category for each of these. If there are any tasks that can be completed within two minutes, give them half an hour to go through these and get each of them done. This can be giving a phone call to confirm something, taking the trash out - anything that is done very quickly. Once this is done, ask your partner what can be delegated. Delegation is a great way of reducing the amount of time that is wasted on tasks that can easily be done by someone else, thereby giving your entrepreneur more time with you or to spend on tasks that truly only he or she can do.

Then, ask them to find the tasks that can be deleted-those are the tasks that don't have to be done, or some that have been on the list for a long time but for which he or she just cannot find the motivation to do. Of course, we are talking about things that can be deleted. For example, completing tax returns cannot be deleted!

Now, all that should be left are the 'defer' tasks: the tasks that need to be done but in the future. This is where prioritization can take place and where you may need more time.

One of the most commonly known ways of prioritizing is called the priority matrix. This is done as follow: Urgent matters are either important or not important and non-urgent matters are either important or not important.

Create a matrix like this for your partner and guide him or her through the process. Sometimes, brainstorming the various tasks that need to be done can help them figure out what really is urgent and what isn't. For example, if tax returns are due within the next few weeks, they would go into the "Urgent and Important" category. On the other hand, if your partner has been planning to write a book for a long time but simply cannot find the motivation, the task can go in the "Not Urgent, Important" section. Usually, you would then prioritize the tasks as follows:

- Urgent and Important
- Not Urgent but Important
- Urgent, but Not Important

- Not urgent, not important

The energy technique refers to the process by which you break down the scheduled tasks in order of energy that is needed to perform them, rather than priorities. Of course, this doesn't mean keeping the things that are most important last, but it means making sure that the necessary tasks can be done based on the amount of energy that your partner has. For example, if they need to do their tax returns, they may have to think about getting this done first thing in the morning to avoid approaching 3PM and having done nothing at all in this regard. If your partner is most productive and works best in the morning, it usually makes more sense to get all the difficult stuff out of the way when they have the most energy, and to get the smaller tasks done later on, once they are lower on energy and attention.

So, ask your entrepreneur to figure out what the priorities are first. Then, schedule time together that will work for them in terms of the energy they have and how much time they can realistically put into every single activity. The key here is truly to be realistic. There is no point in creating a list of priorities that they cannot follow. At the end of the day, all this will do is create much more stress for everyone and make your entrepreneur resent the entire process. So, first, list out all priorities, and second, break these down in order of time and energy needed. This is much more conducive to successful time management and to feeling happy and fulfilled with what they will have accomplished throughout the day! Of course, you should also make sure that all tasks which are due (those that have a specific deadline) come first, no matter how much energy they may require.

Once this has been done, help your entrepreneur create to-do lists every day. Similarly, you may want to spend time together at the beginning of every week (such as Sunday night) to plan your week together. A solid way to do this is by using block scheduling.

Block Scheduling has been growing in popularity over the past few years. As the name suggests, it refers to blocking time on your schedule to specific times. This does not have to be a painful experience! In fact, you can easily enjoy the process simply by doing it in bed, in front of the TV, on Sunday night. Get yourself a cup of tea (or a glass of wine- whatever you prefer!) and start working together on blocking time. With the list of tasks to do, start by writing down every single deadline that is coming up. Color coding also helps with this. For example, use red for urgent things, blue for work-related, green for exercise and workout time, purple for date night, etc.

Once you have all the deadlines written down, work with your partner to figure out exactly how much time is needed for each task. Then, schedule a time to complete each of these. Similarly, your entrepreneur partner should block "catchup" time-this is a grey zone that serves as blocked time for anything they may need to do. For example, if they are in the middle of a meeting and realize that they have to send a business proposition, they can use this block of time instead of having to try and squeeze it during their lunch time.

Although you may want to do this together before you work on prioritizing, it is still important to mention it. Your partner is likely to want to continuously better him or herself by taking on new projects and always expanding their vision. What this means is that their dreams are also likely to be changing as they achieve more and more things. For example, if their previous dream was to make $SOK, once they have reached this, they will need to sit down and figure out what is next on their bucket list. Finding dreams is an exciting process, especially with someone you love and with whom you see yourself growing and becoming a better person. A solid part of this is figuring out the 'why' or the purpose behind one's life and activities. So, do this together. It'll create a bond like no other!

A good way to do so is to look at how far one has gotten. From there on out, your partner may also get the self-confidence boost which is needed for him or her to enlarge their vision, and to start thinking about what can become reality, even if it sounds extremely far-fetched. For example, you can ask your partner questions such as, "If you could get anything you wanted tomorrow, without any hurdle or barrier in your way, what would it be?".

This question gets them to ponder over what is missing from their life right now, and what they would like to experience. Then, you can also discuss what you feel you could do as a couple and how you could experience more amazing things together, whether that's also a bit far-fetched or not. The goal isn't to put barriers in your way already. Instead, the goal is for both of you to figure out exactly what it is that you can and would like to achieve together.

Is this based on what you think would make you feel fulfilled, or on what you know would bring you a sense of fulfillment? This question further asks you and your partner to figure out where this need or want is based. Is this based on something you may have seen on TV? Where is this dream based? What kind of inspiration brought you to think this is what you want? Is it realistic? These questions, once answered, will give you a better idea of your real dream. Is it really to achieve all these things, or is it mostly to achieve the idea of it? Do you want to live in Bali and be a digital nomad? Why? If you saw the unedited pictures and videos of the place (none of the Instagram Influencer stuff), would you still want to? If so, then yes, it's your dream!

In fact, trying to separate yourself from the social media picture of perfection or "dream" life can help both of you separate what your real dream is from what the media tells you it should be. As mentioned in the previous section, your entrepreneur wants to stay away from the status quo in many cases, so how will this be made into a dream and then a reality? Brainstorming together and thinking of all the talents you have as well as the things you are passionate about can help. Similarly, finding out what used to make you unhappy which now makes you happy can also give you an idea of what the dream really is. Brainstorm together, map it out on a board, and start figuring out what the top five things you absolutely want to achieve are. Ask yourself what you would want to have done, no exception, if you had only one day to live. In most cases, this is your next step and the big dream you should be focusing your energies on.

You may have noticed that I put a lot of importance on planning and finding regular times to create schedules and find dreams together in a controlled and stable manner. Well, that's a great way to find and establish stability within the relationship. Once either (or both) of you have control over his or her life in terms of the time needed to perform tasks, using block scheduling, and using the time to find out together what you are working towards, stability will come. Similarly, give yourselves time to check in with one another. Once a week, look at where you are and what you have achieved, and celebrate these achievements. Provide each other with support and congratulate each other for your efforts. Stay on top of your tasks by making sure you dedicate time and effort to planning for your future and for your week and stick by the schedule you have created as much as possible. If it helps, choose one day where you always go out on a date, even if it means grabbing lunch quickly or walking around the park for thirty minutes. Having these specific events set in stone will help both of you have some kind of stability.

In fact, establishing boundaries with one another will help create this stability as well. If you both agree on basic rules for the house and on rules regarding how your relationship works, you can both have specific expectations. It also makes it much easier to figure out when something is not working out the way you have planned it or discussed it. If someone misses a date or forgets about an important event, remind them and make sure you plan it more thoroughly next time. Try and make time for meals with one another- again, this contributes to the routine you can create as a couple and can help create more stability out of two busy people's schedules. As long as you both do your best to stick by what you have agreed upon and you make time to plan out your time together and apart, you will enjoy more stability and predictability in an otherwise very scattered and chaotic relationship.

Ultimately, these should be fun activities to do together! If the thought of having to sit and plan your week, discuss your dreams, and prioritize together sounds like work that you just do not want to do, maybe being with an entrepreneur, or someone who lives based on schedules and always running around trying to find the next most exciting project, is not the best option for you. However, again, you are holding this book, and so I doubt this is the case! Instead, if you are able to show each other your appreciation for one another and can spend time discussing your dreams and aspirations together, you are in for the long run. An important aspect of keeping chis passion going, however, is showing love and affection. And, this is done by using one (or more) of the five love languages.

Chapter Six

Self Sufficiency & Self-Care

Self-sufficiency refers to the state of being completely self-sufficient or sufficing yourself by providing and depending only on yourself. When you are in a relationship, self-sufficiency could also hurt your relationship more than anything. So, this chapter discusses when self-sufficiency is needed, and when emotional support should be used to ensure your relationship is successful and mutually supportive.

As you may have already heard, self-sufficiency and self-love are very much interconnected. Self-sufficiency refers to you being able to rely solely on yourself, whatever circumstance you are in. Entrepreneurs tend to be very self-sufficient in general, namely because they are aware that people will come and go, excitement regarding their new venture will equally come and go, and therefore they must be able to stick to their beliefs and convictions like no one else ever will. Thus, self-sufficiency all starts with the person itself. At the end of the day, no one will ever be able to make you as happy as you can make yourself happy-that is the basis of any healthy relationship. Your partner should be an addition to your life, someone that makes your days better and someone with whom you can share your life, nothing else. Your self-sufficient self will also help you overcome any hardship you may face later if you ever break up as you will have learned not to be dependent on another person.

If you nurture yourself, your own happiness, and your ability to be on your own, you are also nurturing your relationship in a way. The rationale behind this is intricate: if you are able to love yourself the way you are, love your life the way you live it, and you are certain about what you do, no matter what-you can begin to live a life that is more fulfilling as you are self-assured that you are at the right place at the right time.

 On the other hand, if you spend a significant portion of time doubting yourself and your abilities, you may very well end up feeling as though only something or someone can fulfill the need you have to feel better about yourself. Instead, do attempt to work on yourself and your abilities, become extremely confident about the things you can achieve and the things you are great at, and do not rely on others to fulfill this need.

I get it, now you're wondering what? But isn't that the opposite of what you just wrote down? Yes and no. On the one hand, it is true that self-reliance and the ability to fully focus on your own achievements without being dependent or reliant on others is important. it helps you build self-confidence and trust in yourself that is otherwise difficult to come by. Nonetheless, being so self-reliant that you struggle to let other people in can do the opposite, it can make your partner feel like they are not allowed into any part of your life and Like you are keeping them in a box, apart from all other aspects.

Like any other person, an entrepreneur needs emotional support. Not only this, but most entrepreneurs actually enjoy coming home and having to drop the act they have to play where they have everything together. Although yes, it is a lifestyle, it can also get very exhausting. Therefore, being able to come home and just crash on the couch is something any entrepreneur would appreciate, especially if it means getting your emotional support as well.

Entrepreneurs cannot show weakness at work. If they show an ounce of doubt in regards to the work they are doing or the business they are involved in, they also risk losing face, losing investors, and could lose everything else as well. It is for this very reason that being able to open up fully to their partner is a necessity. They don't want to feel like they need to show the best version of themselves to their partner all the time- instead, they want to be able to come home and tell their partner about their day, even if it means complaining and finally being able to show weaknesses.

For example, your entrepreneur partner may finally take the chance to share the difficult clients they had to deal with, or the fact that they are completely overwhelmed by a huge order they got. In this case, being too self-reliant can push them away as it may make them feel like you do not understand them, or like you do not want to share your own stories and weaknesses with them. If you cannot be vulnerable with one another, you may be jeopardizing your success as a couple. This isn't necessarily done on purpose, but it can hurt you and your partner's connection quite drastically.

If you were brought up to be independent and self-reliant, the idea of opening up to someone may feel like you are quite literally taking off your armor and letting yourself be open to the possibility of getting stabbed-not to sound too dramatic. But in all seriousness, being emotionally supportive is something we can all improve on, especially in a time and age where self-obsession is becoming rather glamorized on the internet via social media. So, caring about someone else. How do we do that?

First and foremost, return to our discussion on love languages. Sometimes, all your partner wants is to be told and shown that you care for them. This can mean spending quality time with them or purchasing a gift that you know will mean a lot to them. If you know they have had a really rough time lately at work, doing something kind for them may give them just that extra push they need to feel more appreciated and like they can take on any challenge they may need. If they enjoy self-help books, for example, why not purchase one for them if they feel low? These are the kinds of ways you can show your appreciation.

Modern life is incredibly busy, and between balancing the business needs, family needs, and individual needs, it can often be difficult to remember to make time for our partners. In fact, it can be quite easy to start taking them for granted. This change between them holding a key spot in our lives, to adopting more of a secondary role occurs so gradually that it's hard to see it even happening. In this way, couples need to set aside a little time every day for the essential communication that helps them to remain emotionally connected. Friendship is absolutely essential to a satisfying and stable relationship. We would never dream of greeting our close friends without interested inquiries into their day and their lives. The same should be true for our partners.

Yet the longer two people are together, the further such simple gestures of friendship decline. This decline is not because couples start to dislike each other but because they become too comfortable together. So, taking the time to ask your partner how their day was is a simple way of re-establishing one of the 'friendly' gestures that demonstrate to your partner that you are interested in them, in how their lives are going.

Of course, once you've asked, you also need to be ready to listen. Although asking in itself might already take a lot, especially if you are tired and have had a long day, showing that you care and that you are open to hearing all about his or her struggles will come off as you being a part of your team. Listening means a few things: having a body language that shows openness, for example. Make sure your body is turned towards your partner and keep your body open - try not to cross your arms or your legs. This small change can make a major difference in the way your partner feels about opening up to you.

Similarly, try to stay off your phone. Put it on Do Not Disturb if needed, but make sure that your attention does not seem to be split two ways. By nodding and listening to their words and emotions, you are showing empathy and care, especially if you agree with them and show emotions that send the message "I feel your pain and I am here with you". Try not to interrupt or counterargue what they are saying-it is not always necessary to act like the devil's advocate, especially when someone is sharing their perspective with you. If you don't understand something, or if you feel like a part of their story and feelings are unclear, clarify. Finally, before you try and give advice, try summarizing their feelings and see if you have understood them clearly. Once this is done, you can also ask whether they want advice or if they just need someone to talk to and share their ideas with.

Although we may be tempted to invite them to look at the other side of the story, it is sometimes more helpful to validate how they feel first. Automatically going against what they say and saying, "but have you thought of blah blah blah" may feel like you are disregarding how they feel and are instead trying to say that their perspective of the situation is wrong. If you let them know that you see the situation and understand their perspective of it, you are making sure that they feel like they have been listened to, and not like you are just trying to excuse the behavior or the situation that has happened to them. And yes, even if it is just a small event, if it has impacted your partner negatively, they will still appreciate receiving support. Similarly, if you don't feel like giving advice is the right thing to do -and sometimes that's only appropriate if they specifically ask you for it-, asking "have you ever dealt with this before? Do you know what you can do to make this better?" May sound more welcoming and nice than telling them they should do ABC instead. Being told what to do might not help their feelings. They may only feel like they haven't been listened to, which can just hurt them more and make them feel more alone.

If you feel like they need more emotional support, providing physical affection can also help. Whether this means giving them a hug, or even just letting them lay their head on your lap, it can truly help them to feel like they are being supported in all ways. Avoid making them feel small or like their problem is not all that important. Avoid saying things like, "yes but other people have it worse" or "it's easy to get over the problem don't worry", because saying so may make them feel 1.ike their worries and feelings are being invalidated.

A good way of being emotionally supportive is also helping the person get past the difficulties they are facing by offering them to do something else. Ideally, you would be doing something which requires more physical activity or something that gets them out of the place you are in. For example, go on a run together, go watch a movie, or go get bubble tea together. Help them get their mind off the troubles they are dealing with, but make sure that the problems are not simply ignored or forgotten about. To this end, checking in with the person once they have gotten past the biggest emotional hurdle can be helpful.

They may realize that the situation they were in was not as dramatic as they originally thought it was, and they may have had the mental clarity to get themselves out of the problems. In fact, sometimes, just having someone to talk to about one's problems can help to achieve this mental clarity. So, if you feel like you have helped your partner, that's great! Although entrepreneurs may feel like they always have everything under control, they are also human and face hurdles in life.

Having you there to support them will make a world's difference, even if it means opening yourself up. Ultimately, do not mistake self-reliance for complete independence. You can keep your self-reliance while also being supportive of your partner, and vice versa. On that note, let's now discuss another aspect of dating an entrepreneur: how not to compare your relationship to that of others.

Protecting Your Time, Filling Your Own Cup

I believe that this may be the most important of all subjects. You can't do anyone any good if you are running on empty. If you are working 90 + hours a week and your business owner is working just as much, if you are taking all the responsibility at home and he/she is only focused on the business, if you aren't taking any time for things you enjoy, you are destined to fail. Then you've ignored filling your own cup for so long all of these things take a toll on you and your marriage. It is critical for all people-yes, even you- to take some time to protect and invest in yourself. Go for a walk. Play with your dog. Look for the beautiful in little moments. Remember that you matter to your business owner.

What if you have personal opportunities that don't line up with the goals that you and your business owner agreed upon? It just means, that if it is important enough it will present itself again and the time, money, and space will be made. Don't make the mistake of "keeping score". It'll just make you miserable.

Emotions

Being married to a business owner can mean that your emotions run the gamut within minutes; scared to thrilled, angry to elated, frustrated to productive. Honestly, it can be exhausting. This is why you have to know yourself and your business owner! If your personality is reserved and controlled but his/hers is passionate and extroverted and having a basic conversation leads to fireworks, discussing something more serious could be like lighting dynamite.

While you want to be their cheerleader, if you allow yourself to be pulled in and excited about every idea that crosses your business owner's mind, you'll wear yourself out pretty quickly! My advice? Invest in a good BS meter. Seriously! Be dubious when your person comes jumping up and down about a new idea. Even if they don't really know you are dubious. Don't allow yourself to get too worked up about every idea that is brought to the table. It's important to be supportive, but don't bet the farm on any one conversation.

This is a great opportunity to bring a dose of reality into the world of your business owner. Try to be more even keeled while helping them deal with their own emotions. Business owners are just excitable people! Every new thing can spark a whirlwind of happy, fist pumping joy. You can be happy, but don't start buying the champagne yet. Be their calm in the storm.

While happy business owners are wonderful and fun to be around, there is the other side of the coin too. The business world is fraught with frustration and difficulties. You have to be sure, as the spouse, that you aren't sucked down by their sadness and discouragements. They are allowed their fears. They probably aren't unfounded, but just because they fell in a hole today while working out an idea, doesn't always mean it's the end of the world. It's hard to find a balance between sharing your fears with your partner and working them up even more about a shared fear.

As the spouse, the goal is to maintain a level playing field for our business owner. That's not always easy because we love them and are tied to them. When they hurt, we want to hurt too. But, if you ride their rollercoaster too long, you might find out that what was said as fact was actually just a passing phase/emotion/time. They were up or down for only a minute. That might cause some frustration on your part because you were crying in the closet or calling all your friends and sharing the excitement based on their one minute of emotion. So, get yourself a BS meter that can judge whether this is a "certain doom" scenario or just a bump in the road. You'll thank yourself in the long run, and I promise your business owner will thank you too. Even geniuses need people who stay calm in the midst of their storms. Be that calm!

Chapter Seven

Avoid At All Costs

Comparison

While it is true that we live in a society which is increasingly becoming all about sharing one's experiences and achievements with the rest of the world, it does not necessarily have to mean that you should be comparing yours to those of others. We have all heard it before, comparing ourselves to others only brings pain and jealousy.

Two feelings that quite honestly do not bring much positivity in your life, what if, instead of comparing how your relationship is panning out, you were to focus on the positives that you get to experience throughout your relationship? Of course, there are positive comparisons to make, especially when it comes to being in a toxic relationship. However, if the comparison makes you doubt your very healthy and happy relationship, perhaps it's time to do some introspection to understand where this insecurity in your relationship is rooted.

If you compare your relationship to another which is seemingly doing better, you may be having serious insecurities with your relationship. Perhaps you are looking at couples who are always happy and spending loads of time together, and so you feel bad about your relationship because your partner is often gone on business trips or has very little time to spend with you.

With an entrepreneur, it's no secret that you may end up having a lot of time on your hands to doubt your relationship. Not only this, but as mentioned, your friends and family will either hate or love them, therefore making it difficult for you to ignore the comments others make. What I have outline, however, is also that the people who make many negative relationship comparisons tend to be much less committed to their partners, may be considering other partners, are not as satisfied as other couples, and are sometimes guilty of being neglectful of their partner. Ultimately, these comparisons not only hurt the relationship itself because they insert self-doubt and foster more of it in your relationship, but they also hurt the partner who may have no idea why fights are happening and why their relationship is constantly being compared to others.

Naturally, always comparing your relationship to figure out what others are doing that you aren't doing might be toxic to your relationship. You may just end up feeling like all you do is think about what other people have that you don't, and of course, that can be hurtful. However, there are times where comparisons can be good. For example, if you feel like your partner is not putting in as much effort as he or she should, or if you are starting to doubt whether your relationship may be somewhat toxic, asking yourself about it and comparing the way positive and healthy relationships work to yours could be positive.

The cycle of violence in any relationship is usually easy to spot for an outsider, but for the person living through it, it may be completely impossible to see. Sometimes, we don't realize that the way our partner dismisses our point of view is disrespectful because we are focused on making things work out. For example, you may feel like it is just passion if you fight a lot, and maybe you even wonder if it's because you love each other so much that you end up screaming at each other. However, certain things aren't normal, and certain things shouldn't be normalized within your relationship. If you have doubts and feel like you are not being treated with respect, comparing the way you are treated to how your friends are treated by their partners is the only time you should compare.

A less positive reason to compare your relationship is because you are insecure about the way it is going. Instead of focusing on comparing your relationship to others, the more productive option is to discuss it with your partner. For example, if you are jealous because your friends' partners cake them out on scooter rides at 3AM spontaneously, and you feel like there is that spark and spontaneity missing in your relationship, approach the discussion from a caring perspective.

Share with them that you would like to be more spontaneous and that you are interested in doing new things. Approaching it from a comparative perspective will only create a defensive mood in which your partner feels like he or she needs co ace like someone else to fulfill your needs, which is naturally something that no partner wants to hear. I fully understand that comparison can at times be a natural default setting for some people. It's difficult to not compare our lives to the lives of others, especially when we feel we are missing out on fun and excitement due to the complications of the business.

Stand Against Infidelity and Jealousy

You know the phrase, "with great power comes great responsibility"? Well, there should be another that says, "with great success comes great temptation". Our next step is goal setting and every goal is contingent on a level of trust. If there are trust issues we must continue to communicate our boundaries to set attainable goals. This has to be part of the conversation if we are to reach success. We must clear the air on this sensitive subject before we can get to our next objective.

Late night business meetings are the bane of any business owner. Golf course meetings, overnight travel, out of country travel, meetings at bars and other people's houses all of these things are part and parcel of running a business. You must BE where the investors, mentors, and partners are in order to be WHAT they want. However, there is this little thing called a marriage that often suffers while the business is built. And yes, jealousy happens easily. Once that little monster gets a foothold, it's really hard to shut that door.

So, what do we do? We address it! Don't be afraid to remind your spouse that you are still here, minding the home front, while he/she is out in the trenches of the business world. Don't be afraid to push for relationship building time with your spouse. I know it's hard to see that as a priority when the wolf is at the door, but if you don't make it a habit to be "together" as a couple before success comes, it will be that much harder to do once success happens. Because, my friends, temptation is all around us. And success is a powerful aphrodisiac. It is your job, as the spouse, to let others know that you are not only married to your business owner, but that you will do whatever is necessary to keep that marriage sound, healthy, and thriving.

Remember that jealousy can come from both sides and in many forms. For example, he's jealous because you get to stay home and be "that" person who maintains relationships with family and children. You are jealous because he's leading a jet-set life while globe-trotting around and meeting rich, beautiful, unattached people who can make his dreams come true. Leading two separate lives is a marriage killer!

Having someone to talk to, who is unbiased and unafraid to set the record straight between the two of you, is a wonderful resource. All of those, he said/she said arguments can be settled, if you will actually stop and listen to each other. A counselor can help with that. If a counselor isn't quite your cup of tea, you can find a mentor. Another part of a having a successful marriage, and business, is the ability to troubleshoot with a mentor, someone who has been there and done that.

If you already have a ready-made answer to temptation, you can avoid the pressure of being put in a position to stand your ground in a tempting situation. This can even work to just get out of that additional drink which you know will be the one to send you over the edge- or for other such uncomfortable situations.

I don't care. "My husband/wife is expecting me" can be something relatable or scary, depending on the situation. Let's not mince words. If you and your business owner have already discussed what he/she will do when approached by someone offering a sexual encounter, then when the encounter happens, the answer is already there. Infidelity happens when we least expect it. So, expect the temptation, talk about the solutions, look the lion in the face, and conquer. Don't be a statistic, my friends. Be a success story!

Avoiding infidelity isn't just a moral issue that could tear apart a family. It can ruin a business. One wrong move towards an employee or colleague and you could find yourself ruined and on the wrong side of a lawsuit. That is not the kind of publicity any business can weather.

Jealousy Over the Business

Do you ever get the feeling that you are actually playing second fiddle to the business? As if you are the mistress and the business is the woman? How many of us feel like we are actually not the focus of our business owner? As if we have to sneak around and steal moments for household conversations? This is a huge deterrent for those of us who actually feel like we shouldn't push our business owner to participate in something that doesn't relate directly to the business. And yet, if these conversations don't happen the marriage is essentially a sham.

Chapter Eight

Business Proofing Your Home

For most people, one of the fears as the spouse of a business owner is that they will go broke and have to file for bankruptcy. It's one of the entrepreneur's fears too. In fact, it's one of their number one motivators. Financial security is a sore spot in a lot of marriages. According to Jeff Paper Dew's article, *Thrifty Couples are the Happiest Couples*, the likelihood of divorce increases to 45°/o when one spouse feels that the other spouse isn't managing their communal money well. Having conflicting money values and money styles can cause dangerous disharmony in a marriage. All couples fight about money, because everyone comes into a marriage with their own baggage regarding money.

The best way to manage the dreaded money monster is to get a plan, one that both spouses understand and agree to. Most often, a plan includes a team of experts to help guide decisions so that you're not flying blind. Trusted professionals such as lawyers, accountants, financial planners and bookkeepers are good resources to helping you, as a couple, protect your personal assets. Taking the time to understand the financial landscape that your business provides helps facilitate communication about financial decisions for the family.

On the home front, the first step to understanding the money flow in and out of our home was to schedule a weekly family business meeting. We all like to think that we can just "talk about stuff" whenever we need to talk. But, honestly, this never happens. While the concept of a family meeting might seem formal, the point is that we have to meet our business people where they are at the moment. It says to our spouse that you want to be as important as the rest of the things in their schedule, without sounding pushy or nagging. Scheduling a meeting sets aside time to address issues, prioritize decisions, establish action items, and assign who is to do what. This allows us to equalize responsibility, minimizes surprises, lessens the chance of over commitment or double booking, and helps prevent things from getting lost in the shuffle of life.

At the family business meeting, ask him/her to explain exactly how we get paid. This explanation led to whiteboards and markers, graphs and flowchart documents. All very overwhelming but allowing him to be the "teacher" helped us come together on a cellular level. You shouldn't be penalized for simply wanting to understand and be on the same page as your partner. Comfort levels usually increase with understanding.

Did you grow up with money? Did your spouse? Are you used to having it or not having it? Are you a saver or a spender? What is your spouse's perspective on saving for retirement or college funds for the kids? Or what about this perspective: "Yes, it pays my bills, but I still hate it and resent it". We've all been there, haven't we? Yes, we know that the business brings in money needed for food, clothes, shelter, etc., but there is life beyond just making ends meet. If you don't have a passion for both your marriage and your business, then just paying the bills leaves a lot to be desired in both. You have to want to connect on more than just the bottom line.

They say that money is the root of all evil. When it comes to starting a business, or multiple businesses, your feelings about money and the security it provides can cause issues with your business owner. If you see risk and your business owner sees opportunity, a fight is almost guaranteed. You have to protect yourself and your marriage from the evils that come from NOT talking about money.

With the discussions about long-term and short-term projections for your business, you must also discuss your feelings of vulnerability when your business owner uses "family" money for the business. You must take the bull (or bill) by the horns and address whether you feel a loss of control when finances are changed. You must express these things to your business owner before these decisions are made.

He/she must understand how a risk taken for the business can also seem like a risk taken for the family. Clear and concise conversations need to happen about how and why the "business" finances must be separated from the "household" finances. Don't worry, this is a constantly changing, ever-present conversation that CAN be successfully addressed as long as you and your business owner are willing to come at it with the same end goal in mind; having a successful business AND marriage.

I'm going to take a moment right here to suggest you also read my book, *Mind Your Business: Entrepreneurship 101*. In this book I give all of the legal and establishing steps entrepreneurs should take to protect their family assets from business failures.

Roles and Responsibilities

You must discuss roles within the family; who cooks dinner, who picks up dry cleaning, who feeds the dog? All these things are part of life, but also can become a flash point for a marriage if not discussed first. Communicating the needs of the family in a calm, rational manner before they blow up is critical. Balance is key so that everyone feels supported. You cannot assume that your partner has the same ideas on roles and responsibilities as you. You cannot hold anyone accountable to a standard he or she has not agreed to. There will be task and needs at home, and it is important to communicate your expectations because that beast behind the business is coming for 100% of your time and energy if you let it.

Family/Friends and Their Impact on Your Business

One of the hidden threats to any business comes from a source that you probably haven't considered. I know maybe you hadn't considered that before, but you cannot be friends with just anyone when you or your partner own a business. We all have friends and family. Ironically enough, these family members and friends don't consider our business before they go out and interact with the world. Again, shocking!

Sometimes these family members and friends go out and do things that might reflect negatively on your business. They don't mean to, of course- well, some of them do. What matters is how you handle it. You may see people out in the community with whom you have a personal relationship; sister, hairdresser, dog groomer, pooper scooper, drunk uncle, etc. You might employ a person who has made bad decisions in their personal life; coming to work drunk or high, staying out all night partying, etc. You have to decide how to address these things before they happen. Set precedent early for addressing bad behaviors. I wouldn't recommend calling these people out in public or Facebook shaming them online. The fact is we all have such people in our lives and it's likely we can't or won't end our personal relationships with them. So, how do you handle your relationships without embarrassment or damage to your reputation? That's an ongoing question and one you and your business owner need to discuss before the damage to the business or relationship is so massive that it's irreconcilable. Truthfully, most strong business can weather these little storms and they eventually blow over. Riding the rollercoaster that is business life is part of the fun.

All in the Family

On the subject of emotion, I feel that this is as good a time as any to address nepotism. I seriously cannot tell you the damage this can cause to your extended family and in your social circle by hiring family.

In my opinion, it is a bad, bad idea. Some family businesses manage just fine, but it can become very messy. The idea of this book is how to keep your family steady in the midst of the sea of business, and hiring friends and family is sure to rock the boat. Family will believe that they can keep it behind office walls, but it will trickle down and infect your family. Proceed with caution!

Chapter Nine

Communication 101

Couples must learn to have "I feel" conversations instead of "What you did" arguments. When we take the position of simply constantly arguing behavior we never quite get anything accomplished. However, when someone who loves you hears that you feel poorly, it stops them in their tracks. That is the power of love. That is also the power of effective communication.

Communication can drastically improve how you connect with your partner and your mutual expectations. Communication involves more than just speaking to your significant other in a way that you would like to be communicated with, but it also involves making sure that you are on the same page when it comes to what you expect from one another. As mentioned throughout the previous chapters, dating an entrepreneur is something that can become emotionally exhausting if you are not clear on what you expect from one another. For example, you may feel like you are constantly running after your partner, or like you are waiting for them to update you on where they are standing in the relationship. This can, of course, be frustrating. And, after a while, you may simply be sick and tired of it. However, if there is no communication between the two of you regarding this matter, it can be very difficult for you both to understand what you expect from one another and what your expectations are.

Therefore, communicating and understanding what you want from each other is a way to make sure your relationship remains a healthy and thriving one. This chapter will outline ten ways to have good communication in a relationship. But first, remember what we discussed in the previous chapters: set boundaries with your entrepreneur! Boundaries have been brought up many times throughout the book. It is a very important element in any relationship. This will ensure that you are both clear on what's expected and what works or doesn't work in your relationship.

Find the Right Timing

When it comes to starting a conversation about the things that are on your mind, timing is everything. If you see your entrepreneur, come home looking disheveled and very tired at 10PM, perhaps it's not the right time to proceed with difficult conversations.

Use "I" Statements

This is typical advice given to any couple, friend group, or even family member when it comes to communicating. I-statements refer to statements that start with "I". For example, you could explain that you feel like your entrepreneur partner has not been giving you as much attention as usual and that you miss them. Or you could also mention that you feel like you aren't connecting as well as usual and that it is hurting your feelings. Instead of using words that sound like they are accusatory or using language that sounds like you are constantly blaming your entrepreneur partner for not doing the right thing, it would be best to use language that uses "I" statements so that your discussion feels like this - a discussion - and not as a conflict automatically.

Be Willing to Compromise and Negotiate

Next up, be aware that you will need to compromise to be able to communicate well with your partner. As mentioned previously, your entrepreneur is someone who thrives by always pushing forward new ideas and always wanting to be right. Sometimes it will be difficult for the both of you to come to an agreement because they may feel like they aren't being heard unless you dearly show that you do understand where they are coming from. So, the both of you will need to be ready to compromise. By compromising on a solution that you both feel comfortable with, you can then focus on achieving a solution that is satisfactory for both of you.

Update One Another

It might sound obvious, but many people will tend to forget about this - try to keep each other in the loop! Sometimes, communication can be made much simpler and much more effective if you both know exactly what you are expecting from one another and if you both communicate in your own ways. For example, leaving a note or sending a quick text to your partner to let them know where you are, what you are doing, or what your schedule is like during the day can help you both feel like you are connected to each other even if you are not necessarily together physically. Checking-in during the day can increase how connected you feel, even if you are not physically together, or even though you may not get the chance to talk much during that time.

Leave The Past In The Past

Even though you may try as much as possible to use I-statements and to calm yourself down before you have a big discussion, it is not unlikely that certain conflicts arise and that you feel like nothing you do can help the situation get better. Even if that's how you feel, do not dig up the past. There is no point in trying to find problems that have occurred in the past and trying to dig these back up as ways to get back to your partner. Bringing up more issues that have already been solved only feels like you are grasping at straws.

You're Too Old for Passive Aggressive Behaviors

We all know what it's like to come home and feel like the atmosphere in the room is far from welcoming. Perhaps you walk through the door and your significant other looks at you with a somewhat annoyed look, but no matter how you try to phrase your question to figure out if they are okay, you can't get an honest answer from them. This kind of passive-aggressive behavior does nothing other than make the environment in which you live very improper for productive conflict and communication.

For example, if your partner is late to an event, you both agreed to attend together, instead of making jokes about their delay, you could express it clearly and mention "I am disappointed with your lack of punctuality. You know this is important to me and I am sad about being late because it feels like you do not care as much as I do". Saying a joke about how they're always late won't help the situation because your partner probably already knows that you are annoyed about their delay.

In the same line of thought, giving your partner the silent treatment is just as ineffective. It may make them fear talking to you about their reasons for their actions and instead of provoking a resolution that can lead to a positive outcome (because resolutions do not always end up positively), it will just delay the fight and add fuel to the fire. Communication entails more than just sharing your ideas and perspectives, it also means having the maturity to express how you feel and what you think needs to be changed so that your relationship is more successful. The silent treatment does not allow this to happen.

If you live with other people (like an apartment building), avoid making passive aggressive comments about your partner to others while they are around. This has a similar effect as bullying, and instead of helping your relationship thrive, it may make your partner feel like you are constantly speaking about them to your neighbors, which can worsen your connection, make him or her doubt the seriousness of your relationship, and can very simply lead them to feel unloved.

Clear and direct communication is best, especially with entrepreneurs. They value honesty and people who are frank as it is a much more efficient way of dealing with problems. They forgot to wash the dishes? Remind them. Is this the seventh time in a row that this has happened? Communicate with them and ask them why they think it's the case. Together, you can find a solution that works for both of you and that makes the dishes issue an obsolete one.

Don't Be Dismissive

Dismissing problems and issues that you do not feel comfortable with and sweeping them under the rug won't help your relationship. Instead, it will only delay the imminent conflict. A dismissive attitude can be anything along the lines of "whatever it's fine" to "you won't even change anyways" - two ways to tell your partner indirectly that you don't think the changes are worth making because there's no point.

Of course, this is not at all conducive to a productive conflict that helps you communicate and connect well with one another. Ignoring the issues and problems you are facing will not give you the time and space you need to expand as a couple. For your relationship to last in the long term, you must both be willing to compromise and need to know when you may need to put aside each of your egos in order to enjoy more happiness as a couple overall. Don't ignore issues and don't let your negative emotions build up to the point that you cannot ignore them anymore. That is when explosive arguments and emotions come out. Instead, try to focus on how you can discuss the problems in a way that makes both of you feel listened to and respected.

Another aspect of a dismissive attitude is using aggressive language to try and get your point across. Raising your voice, blaming the other partner or being very critical of their actions, can swiftly turn into verbal abuse. Trying to control or dominate the conversation throughout can similarly make the experience of conversing with one another much worse, which can lead to conflicts that cannot be overcome. Remember: a major portion of the conversation has to be spent listening to the other and understanding their point of view. Even if you are unhappy with their answer or feel like they do not have the right outlook, you should still respect them enough to show understanding and comprehension for their view of the situation.

Focus on What You Feel Verses What Happened

Before you go into any kind of conflict or conversation with your entrepreneur, it's important that you first have a good grasp of how you are feeling. If there is something specifically bothering you, try to first understand what exactly is bothering you and why this is bothering you. Is this something that has occurred many times? Are there other external reasons that could be fueling this annoyance, such as being under a lot of stress, or because it is the result of many other small issues that have added up and led to this bigger problem? Again, remember not to bottle things up. By understanding first how you feel about the situation and why you feel a certain way, you will have a much better understanding of the rationale behind this issue. The clearer you are on your own feelings about the situation, the easier it will be to remain poised and calm when trying to explain your point of view. Similarly, taking a minute to calm down and relax before the conversation can help put things into perspective

Stop Running Away

No matter how comforting it may feel to walk away from a conflict or to slam the door, this is not a way to communicate that is likely to help your relationship. If you feel so angry or overwhelmed with emotions, take a time out. Take the time to regain your composure and to have a moment to yourself to figure out why you feel a certain way. Let your partner know that you need some time on your own in order to feel more in control of your reactions and to avoid saying things you do not mean, but do not simply walk out of the conversations. There's no other way to say it: it's plain disrespectful and your partner deserves to have your respect, even when you are fighting (and vice versa, of course).

Don't Lose Respect for One Another

Closing off on a similar topic, make sure to remain respectful of one another during the conflict. Hold off from using sarcasm or putting your partner down as even though you may think that using humor will help break down the conflict, it may only fuel it further if your partner feels like you are not listening to them the way they wish you would.

Make sure you give each other your undivided attention by putting your phones away and using the right body language. If either of you seem to be disinterested or disconnected from the conversation, question whether it may not be a bad time to be having it.

Use eye contact and abstain from swearing at each other, no matter how angry you may be. What is the bottom line? Be respectful to each other, and before you say things you regret, ask yourself whether your 'tomorrow self' is likely to regret having said certain things.

The same way you should be careful about the way you speak to your partner and when you choose to do so, your partner should also have the same decency. And yes, although entrepreneurs may have very specific ways of acting and may be impulsive or so dedicated to their work and 'grind', it does not excuse their bad behavior if they do not treat you with respect.

Chapter Ten

Evolving Evolution

If there is one thing that I have learned in life, it is that anything alive is always evolving. The business will evolve, and your partner will evolve. That is the whole point of pursing dreams. It evolves us. It's impossible to stare your insecurities in the face every day and still chase greatness without evolving.

Relationships crumble, when we stop giving our spouse or partners room to evolve. Things go south very fast when we become certain that he or she will never grow or evolve. There is a difference between wanting to change someone and having faith that we all grow. For the success of your relationship and business, you have to be open to the idea that how it began may not be how it evolves. You're going to find your partner constantly restructuring the business as he or she learns it. Just as you will find yourself having to love a different version of your partner. The person he or she was twenty years ago will never exist again.

You have to be deliberate in learning and relearning them every day, without fear of how the evolution will impact you. To prepare yourself of the evolutions to come, it is important that you fully learn your partner (and the business) now, today.

Who Are They?

What do you know about your spouse's business? Is it retail, wholesale, technology, construction, a restaurant, cyber security? The options are endless. It is critically important that the spouse of the business owner knows a little about what it the business is all about. If your business owner spends 80+ hours a week doing something that you know nothing about, how in the world can you expect to have a common goal?

Whether he/she acknowledges this or not, you must make them understand that in order for your marriage to be successful, you WANT to know what makes them tick and why they are so passionate about their business. No one became an entrepreneur because of wanting to work less. In fact, most entrepreneurs work an insane number of hours-

-probably more than 60 a week. Even when entrepreneurs aren't actually working, they're at least thinking about the business3". If your business owner is spending that much time on their business, don't you think you should know a little about it? If you haven't already, spend some time getting to know the ins and outs of your spouse's business.

The key is communication and a mutual understanding that both of your voices are important when making big decisions that affect the family. There are ways of doing this that communicate respect and support to your spouse, but it must be handled delicately because these strong personalities are very used to running the show and having people just do what they tell them to. The first step to empathy is having a mutual understanding that you are as uncomfortable in their domain as they are in yours. Not everything has to be a mutual decision, but respecting each other's input goes a long way to smooth over hurt feelings of inequality. If you're wondering, screaming the phrase "I AM NOT YOUR EMPLOYEE!" does not go over well in an argument.

The bottom line is this: business owners have interesting personalities, which can cause clashes in a marriage. Both of you should take a personality assessment. Personalities shape worldviews and thought processes. Becoming acquainted with your respective personality types may lead to a better understanding of one another. Get to know yourself and your partner and you will be much better equipped to handle what the business and the marriage throw at you.

Who Are You Inside and Outside of the Business?

Welcome to the soul-searching portion of my book! Yes, who you are and what you want ARE important to the success or failure of your business owner's business. YES, you matter! And, yes, it matters to your business owner as much as it matters to you. Be honest, were you a person with your own tastes, talents, career, dreams, and hopes before your marriage? The answer, of course, is yes. You had all these things prior to marriage and it's important for you to maintain these aspects of your life. You have value on your own. Your spouse also had these things. He/she also had dreams and hopes before you married. The important part of marriage is that you take yours and his/hers and combine them to form new hopes and dreams. In order for that to happen, you need to each take a long look inside and remember what those things were and then share them with each other.

Just as important as your dreams and hopes are your personality traits that form your personhood- the uniqueness that is YOU. Are you an introvert? Do you like meeting new people? Are you a risk taker? These things matter and if you don't know the answer, as we said earlier there are lots of online tests that you can take to help figure these things out. It's important to know these things about your business owner too. Entrepreneurs are never attracted to individuals with no goals or desires. People who have no dreams of their own will never understand the cost of your dreams.

Chapter Eleven

Bedroom > Boardroom

Let's just be honest. A drought will happen. There will be a season in which the romance and connectivity seems almost nonexistent. It happens for all couples, and it happens even more often for couples that are business owners. Both parties must always understand that the success of the boardroom will never be greater than the success in the bedroom. If one does not find happiness, affection, and love at home, the disconnect will appear at work. Challenge yourself to fall back in love with your spouse this month with these tips.

Be a mystery.

Get closer by finding some distance in your marriage. Make a rule that for the first ten minutes of any night out, you will not discuss the "business" of your relationship: no kid talk, no work recap. You may just remember what having a fun conversation is like again!

Take TV up a notch.

There is nothing wrong with vegging out with your man after a long day, but if Monday through Thursday evenings always consist of little more than zoning out to the DVR or doing separate activities side-by-side, tweak your lazy, chill time to make it more loving. How about a movie in bed with a bowl of popcorn? Or his-and-her backrubs while you watch your favorite show? Or if you can squeeze it into your schedule, after the kids are in bed, put away the tub toys and enjoy a bath together.

Stop calling your spouse "hey."

As in, "Hey, can you pick up the kids after work?" or "Hey, did you remember to call the accountant?" One of the easiest ways to rekindle your romance is to act like you did way back when you were dating. Try a pet name that you used in the early years of your relationship, or the simply more affectionate "Hon's" and "Babe's" that you may not have uttered in years.

Make a top 10 list.

Spend a few moments jotting down your greatest hits from your years together — from the biggies, like your wedding day, to the smaller memories, like the song you played over and over on a camping trip one year. Surprise your partner with the list — leave it on the bed, email it, sit down after dinner and read it together. The exercise will give you an important reminder of why you picked each other in the first place.

Fall in love... with yourself.

It may sound counter intuitive, but one of the best ways to increase the passion within your relationship may be to find new ways to develop yourself outside of it. You can't feel love for someone else if you're feeling crappy about your own life. Arrange a dinner date with a friend. Take a yoga class. Actually cook one of the meals in your "someday" recipe file (or your Pinterest board). Taking care of yourself will replenish you, making you more receptive to love in your life.

Shake it up.

Dozens of studies have found that one of the best ways to bust a rut is by injecting some novelty into your usual routine. Find a free weekend this month, drop the typical Saturday chores-and-errands dance, and plan something that you'll love doing together. Maybe it's as involved as a weekend B&B trip, or maybe it's as simple as spending an afternoon playing tourist in your hometown — say, by checking out the new neighborhood sushi place or visiting a nearby historical site.

Shake up your sex schedule.

We all know that waiting until the end of the night to have sex often means you fall asleep before you get to it. Try alternative times to have sex — your lunch hour, on a Saturday afternoon when the house is empty or by slipping into your spouse's morning shower. If evenings are truly the only available time, make it a priority — get into bed earlier, forego the flannel PJs and make an event out of it.

Practice acceptance.

Nope, your partner doesn't bring home flowers like your best friend's guy. But there are a bazillion ways that your spouse is loving in his own way: rubbing your back after a long day, making Saturday morning pancakes, making up ridiculous songs for your kids. You're more likely to fall back in love with your partner if you're not trying to turn a cat into a dog.

Give your partner a squeeze.

Pop quiz: Have you touched your spouse today? If the only physical contact that you have with the person to whom you're married on a typical day is a quick peck on the cheek before work or bed — it's time to get your act together. That doesn't have to mean upping your game to wild bedroom acrobatics, though, try simply hugging for thirty seconds. Hugging has been proven to boost levels of oxytocin, a hormone that increases feelings of bonding, particularly in women.

Take the one-a-day challenge.

The habit of criticism is hazardous to any relationship, and no one can happily survive in a marriage if they feel more judged than admired. Limit yourself to one criticism a day, figuring out which one matters most is a good exercise. Practice saying that criticism in three sentences or less. Do this over time and you'll see each other in a more positive light and likely rediscover why you fell in love in the first place."

Hang out with your partner's friends.

Yes, really. Seeing your significant other through his or her buddies' eyes can reveal endearing facets of their personality that you might not have seen in a while, or maybe ever — how he or she can tell a joke that brings down the whole room, how kind he or she is when he's having a conversation with someone they just the met, or the way that they (surprise!) brags about you.

Stop giving unsolicited advice.

Okay, so maybe you do know the correct, more efficient way to do everything, but what matters in a marriage is not who's right, but that each person is dedicated to contributing to each other's happiness. Give him the space to learn through trial and error, even if you have to leave the room when he's struggling to cut a tomato for the salad or put a snowsuit on your flailing toddler" It's not your job to correct your spouse.

Fake it 'till you make it.

Yes, after your long day of hurtling work obstacles and wrangling kids, acting sweet and loving might sound as appealing as a jury duty summons, but when you let yourself off the hook every night, your relationship suffers. Don't wait until the spirit genuinely moves you to warm your partner's heart. Just like we can act courageously when we're afraid, we can act lovingly and focus on the positive when we're feeling...well, not quite that way. Today, act like you're madly in love: hug, kiss, call just to say hello, send a loving text. You might be surprised how your partner's response reverses your mood.

Schedule weekly date nights.

Researchers at the University of Virginia have found that couples who spend uninterrupted time together at least once a week have better communication, higher sexual satisfaction, and stronger feelings of commitment than couples who don't. Get out your calendars and schedule weekly couple time for the next month in the same way you would schedule other appointments.

Stop talking about the kids.

Yes, they are the light of your lives. Of course, you can hardly remember what life was like before they came along. But the best thing you can do for them is to develop a strong marriage, and the best way to do that is to spend regular time simply focusing on each other. Set some ground rules to make it easy: Maybe it's that you don't discuss the kids on date nights or after they've gone to bed during the week. Your entire family will be better off if you take some "just the two of us" time to talk about the grownup stuff.

Do something active.

Working towards a common goal builds feelings of togetherness and doing something physical — whether it's training for a half-marathon together or vowing to each lose ten pounds — gives you each an opportunity to encourage and call on each other for support. Spend a Sunday afternoon hiking a nearby park, try a walk after dinner three times this week, or investigate active vacations you might try.

Be realistic about relationship highs and lows.

Stop worrying that "the feeling is gone" and remember that even the best marriages get stuck sometimes, and if you're focused on what's wrong instead of bringing your best self to your marriage, that's a good recipe for failure. Lose the Woe is me" and make a list of the things you can do to make yourself happier right now — and do some of them! "The best way to love your partner is to work on yourself.

Check in.

Yes, you might talk to your spouse 100 times a day, but if you're like most couples, those chats often become more logistical than loving: "Who's picking up milk on the way home?", "What are the weekend plans with your in-laws?". Taking time to do a daily check-in when you really talk will remind you that you're partners in love, not just in the business of running a household. Here's how to do it: Set an alarm on your phone to go off at a certain time in the evening, and when it does, stop whatever you're doing — folding the laundry, answering emails, watching TV and take ten minutes to chat. The best way to start? A simple "How are you?"

Spy on your partner.

Spend five minutes simply observing your spouse when they don't know you're watching and mentally check off ten things you love about him or her. This will remind you of all the little things that made you fall in love.

Absence makes the heart grow fonder.

Literally! There's a reason why the old sentiment is such a classic. Spending time apart gives you a chance to reflect on your relationship, gets you out of your routine and, most obviously (and perhaps most significantly!), gives you an opportunity to miss each other! Get on the phone and schedule that girls' weekend that you and your friends keep talking about, visit your mother or give yourself the gift of some time alone. A little bit of time spent apart will make a big difference in how you reconnect afterwards.

Ask your spouse to teach you something.

We all need to feel needed, and one easy way to show how much you value your partner — and increase loving feelings between the two of you — is by requesting his or her expertise. What does he know that you'd like to understand? How to score a baseball game? How to take a decent photo without relying on the auto setting? How to make his family's famous gumbo recipe? Ask him to show you what he knows.

Don't try to read minds.

Sometimes, our biggest problems with our partners stem from the stories we invent in our heads. Instead of stomping around angry because you assume that your spouse never wants to go out or that he or she doesn't appreciate the things you do around the house — ask how he or she actually feels. An easy cure for your resentment is to stop assuming the worst, and the only way to feel better is to actually talk it out.

Invent an anniversary.

Sure, you celebrate the Big One every year, but why not devise other reasons to mark the passing of your lives together? Reenact your first date by making the same sort of food you ate at the restaurant or rent the movie that you saw together in the theater. Make the first of the month "picnic on the family room floor" night. Have "half" anniversaries by celebrating the date six months before your actual anniversary. By giving ordinary days special significance, you'll give each other reason to stop time and reflect on the life you're building together.

Communicate in a new way.

Are quick texts and post-work check-ins your most common modes of communication? Shake up the way you connect by doing things differently: Send the kind of long, chatty email you send to a girlfriend. Interrupt evening reading to have a chat. In other words, talk for the sake of talking. It will help you remember that along with everything else, your spouse is also your best friend who you really like to talk to.

Create a sexy wish list.

Bedroom routine a little too, well, routine? Make a risqué list of all of the things you'd like for your partner to do to you and leave it in a place where they would never expect it (and no one else will find it!). Your sex life will get a boost because you'll get exactly what you want, but the added element of how and when it happens will make it even hotter.

Go through old pictures.

Simply browsing shots from your history together will help you remember why you fell in love with your partner in the first place. But if you want to take it a step further, examine your "relationship archives" together and reminisce about the memories, large and small, that you've created over the years, whether it's the dozens of photos that you took during your first few weeks as parents or the random candids that you've forgotten about. Going down memory lane can help you...

Have a big night out.

You do not need another date night that involves discussing the kids from the minute you walk out the door until the minute you pay the sitter. You do not need another date night that involves periodic check-ins with your work email. What you do need is to make plans to have the kiddos cared for, and then meet your significant other at a great bar (there's something about arriving there alone that is so much sexier than heading out together) and let loose like you did when you were dating.

Mirror what's missing.

So your spouse isn't romantic. Your partner doesn't say thank you and isn't affectionate. But are you? Examine your biggest gripes about your spouse and turn the spotlight on yourself: When's the last time you really kissed? How long has it been since you called him or her at work just to say hello? When you want more connection, suggest an activity. Instead of communicating about communication, talking about how you don't talk, just try talking. Be proactive and you might find that the easiest route to getting what you want is to simply make it happen.

Discovering something new about what he or she thinks and feels will help you realize that you don't, in fact, already know everything there is to know about him — and help you look forward to all there is yet to come.

COMING SOON

BY

DR. FREDERICK D. ACKLIN

For bookings, bookings, and more updates from

Dr. Frederick Acklin

please visit

https://lergempowerment.org/